A Patient's Guide to
Male Sexual Dysfunction™

Tom F. Lue, MD

Professor of Urology

University of California
School of Medicine

San Francisco, California

Published by Handbooks in Health Care Co.,
Newtown, Pennsylvania, USA

International Standard Book Number: 1-884065-82-1

Library of Congress Catalog Card Number: 99-68558

A Patient's Guide to Male Sexual Dysfunction™. Copyright© 2000 by Handbooks in Health Care Co., a Division of AMM Co., Inc. All rights reserved. Printed in the United States of America. No part of this book may be used or reproduced in any manner whatsoever without written permission, except in the case of brief quotations embodied in critical articles and reviews. For information, write Handbooks in Health Care, 3 Terry Drive, Suite 201, Newtown, Pennsylvania 18940, (215) 860-9600.

Website: www.HHCbooks.com

Table of Contents

Introduction 5

Chapter 1
**What Causes Impotence
(Erectile Dysfunction/ED)?** 8

Chapter 2
Finding the Cause 20

Chapter 3
Treatment Options 29

Chapter 4
Making a Choice 52

Chapter 5
**Other Conditions that
May Cause Erectile Dysfunction** 56

Chapter 6
Finding the Right Doctor 64

Chapter 7
Patient Case Studies 71

Glossary 88

Index 91

This book has been prepared and is presented as a service to the medical community. The information provided reflects the knowledge, experience, and personal opinions of Tom F. Lue, MD, Professor of Urology, University of California School of Medicine, San Francisco, California.

Donna L. Miceli, a medical writer, assisted in the research and writing of this book.

This book is not intended to replace or to be used as a substitute for the complete prescribing information prepared by each manufacturer for each drug. Because of possible variations in drug indications, in dosage information, in newly described toxicities, in drug/drug interactions, and in other items of importance, reference to such complete prescribing information is definitely recommended before any of the drugs discussed are used or prescribed.

Introduction

Male erectile dysfunction (ED), more commonly known as impotence, is defined as a consistent inability to achieve an erection, or to maintain an erection long enough to successfully complete sexual intercourse. ED doesn't affect sexual desire or the ability to have an orgasm. Men can be impotent without experiencing diminished passion, and they can still achieve orgasm. Most men experience temporary impotence on occasion. This can be caused by fatigue, stress, lack of privacy, physical injury, depression, illness, or medication side effects. An occasional episode of impotence is not a major concern. However, when impotence becomes persistent, it can seriously harm a man's self-image and sexual life.

Unfortunately, because most men see the ability to perform sexually as a measure of their masculinity—the term impotence, by definition, implies a 'lack of power'—they are usually embarrassed and reluctant to discuss their impotence with anyone, including their physician. In fact, many men who become impotent won't even admit it to themselves. Also, sadly, many physicians neglect to ask their patients about sexual matters when taking a medical history or performing a routine physical examination.

If you are experiencing frequent episodes of impotence, you probably feel very much alone. You may believe many of the myths about impotence: it's an inevitable part of aging; it's a sign that you've lost your manhood; it's all in your head; you should keep it to yourself; and, worst of all, you can do nothing about it. By choosing to read this book, you've taken the first step toward debunking these popular myths. Above all else, you need to know two very important things:

- You are not alone.
- Most impotent men can be helped.

Because of differences in the way it is defined and the general reluctance to discuss it, the actual prevalence of impotence is difficult to determine. Estimates from a National Institutes of Health (NIH) panel indicate that the number of men in the United States with erectile dysfunction ranges from 10 million to 20 million. Some recent estimates place the number of American men and their partners affected by impotence as high as 30 million. Although impotence is not an inevitable or irreversible consequence of aging, about one third of men who suffer from some degree of impotence are over age 60.

Impotence is treatable in all age groups but, unfortunately, only about 10% of men seek treatment. However, awareness of the treatability of impotence has recently grown and, with the recent U.S. Food and Drug Administration (FDA) approval of the first oral treatment for impotence, men are becoming increasingly aware that they no longer have to live with impotence.

Reading this book is not meant to substitute for a visit to your physician. This book is designed to help you understand the process involved in achieving an erection, the causes of impotence, the various treatments that are available, the resources available for diagnosis and treatment, and what to expect in the doctor's office. Armed with this information, we hope you'll feel more comfortable consulting a physician and taking that first step toward finding a treatment that may help you return toward normal sexual activity.

The author wishes to thank his patients and colleagues for their encouragement and suggestions, which gave birth to many of the new ideas and innovations in this book. The following is an example.

Dear Dr. Lue,

I want to take a moment to thank you for giving me the opportunity to change my life. As a result of my accident, I was unable to gain an erection for 14 years. Because of your research and subsequent treatment program I can now have normal sexual relations on a regular basis. In some respects it is actually better than normal due to the increase in staying power.

In the past I felt insecure and socially alienated by my problem. Thanks to you, I have regained a tremendous amount of self-confidence which, I believe, has had a positive impact on all aspects of my life. My self-image has improved, my levels of stress reduced and, consequently, my attitude towards life in general markedly enhanced.

It is good once again to feel like a man.

Best regards,

Chapter 1

What Causes Impotence (Erectile Dysfunction/ED)?

S exuality is such a natural function of the human condition that few men ever think much about the actual process involved in achieving an erection. Just like the television or the computer, most of us don't think or care about how it works, as long as it works. However, understanding how erections occur is an important step toward diagnosis and treatment for impotence.

Anatomy of an Erection

The process leading to an erection begins with erotic stimulation, which can be triggered by the senses—touch, sight, scent, sound—or by memory. The nervous system responds by sending messages to the pelvic area that cause the smooth muscles inside the penis to relax. The blood vessels widen (Figures 1 and 2), increasing the blood flow into two sponge-like cylinders known as the *corpora cavernosa*, which run along the length of the penis on both sides above the *urethra*, the passageway for semen and urine (Figures 1 and 2). As the corpora cavernosa fill with blood, they expand and press against the veins that would normally drain blood from the pe-

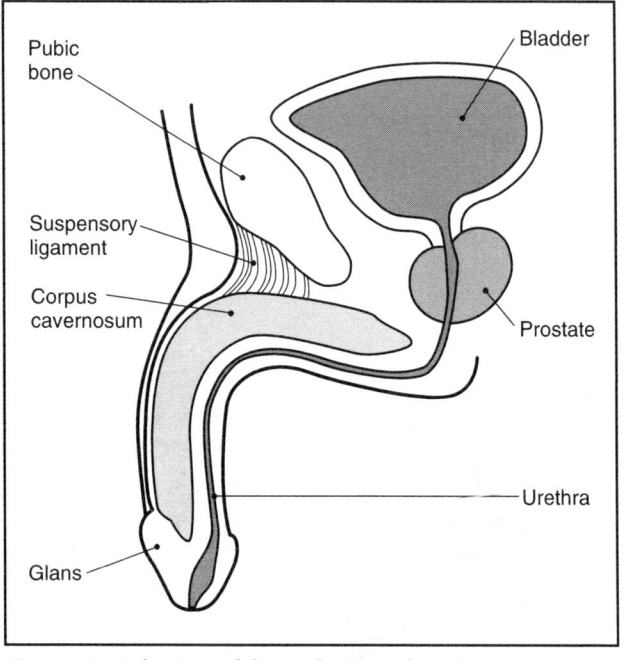

Figure 1: *Side view of the male genital and urinary organs.*

nis. This causes the penis to swell and lengthen, producing an erection. The penis remains erect as long as sexual stimulation continues. After ejaculation occurs, or when sexual arousal passes, the blood drains out of the corpora cavernosa and the penis returns to its normal, nonerect size and shape.

Achieving a successful erection involves the coordinated actions of your brain, blood vessels, nervous system, and hormones. If something affects one of these functions, or interferes with the delicate balance among them, impotence can result.

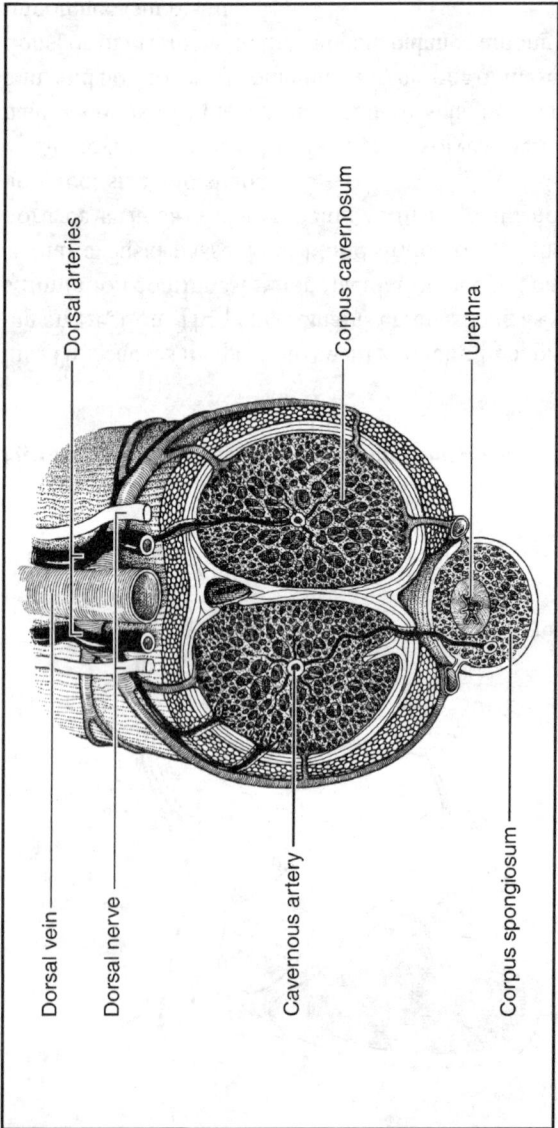

Figure 2: Crossview of the internal structure of the penis. (Used with permission from Walsh PC, Retik AB, et al, eds: Campbell's Urology, 7th ed. Philadelphia, WB Saunders, 1997 Chapter 38).

Until fairly recently, emotions were thought to cause more than 90% of impotence cases. However, doctors have recently determined that a combination of physical and psychological factors are responsible for most cases. Physicians generally divide the causes of erectile dysfunction (ED) into three categories:

- Psychological
- Physical
- Mixed origin—both psychological and physical

Psychological Causes of Impotence

Approximately 10% to 15% of ED cases are purely psychological, which can make diagnosis particularly difficult. Psychological impotence usually occurs suddenly, triggered by such things as stress, anxiety, depression, guilt, low self-esteem, or fear of failure. Marital conflict or a strained relationship with a partner, ignorance about anatomy and sexual function, and strong religious beliefs also can be factors that contribute to impotence.

Most men experience temporary periods of impotence at some time in their lives. It's important not to assume that an episode of impotence signals a permanent problem, and thus will happen again during your next sexual encounter. Because your thought processes are important in successfully achieving an erection, negative thinking can actually cause the problem. If you do experience an episode of impotence, it's best to just forget it and assume that your next sexual encounter will be successful.

If you're experiencing occasional or persistent periods of ED, it's also important to think about the effect it has on your sexual partner. To some degree, most women consider their partner's erection, or lack of erection, as a reflection of their own desirability. Although impotence

Table 1: Physical Causes of Impotence

Erectile dysfunction can be caused by a variety of physical and psychological conditions. The causes and frequency of physical (organic) impotence seen in a typical urology clinic are listed below.

Diseases of blood vessels	33%
Diabetes	25%
Radical pelvic surgery	10%
Trauma, including spinal cord injury	8%
Prescription drugs	8%
Substance abuse	7%
Endocrine problems	6%
Multiple sclerosis	3%
Total:	100%

is only rarely caused by a lack of interest, a man's impotence can damage a woman's self-image if her partner doesn't make it clear that she is desirable.

Physical Causes of Impotence

As many as 75% of all cases of ED can be attributed to underlying medical conditions. Impotence that is caused by a physical problem generally develops gradually, and is characterized by any of the following:

- a failure to initiate, which results from impaired release of the chemical messages that the nervous system sends to the pelvic area, or from lack of interest because of a hormone imbalance;
- a failure to fill, which results from poor blood flow to the penis, caused by blocked arteries;

- a failure to store, which results from blood escaping too quickly from the penis back into the body, caused by atrophy or scarring within the penis.

Table 1 lists the physical causes of impotence.

The Nervous System

The nervous system, which includes the brain, spinal cord, and peripheral nerves, is important in achieving an erection. Any disease or condition that affects the nervous system can cause impotence (Table 2). Conditions that damage the brain, such as Parkinson's disease and Alzheimer's disease, stroke, tumor, and head trauma, have been associated with ED, as have conditions affecting the spinal cord, such as multiple sclerosis, spina bifida, a ruptured disk, tumor, or trauma.

Peripheral neuropathy, which is caused by damage to the network of nerves used for all movements and sensations, is another possible cause of ED. It is commonly associated with such conditions as diabetes, alcoholism, aging, chronic renal (kidney) failure, lupus, and AIDS, as well as exposure to industrial toxins and deficiencies in vitamins B_1, B_2, and B_6. In addition, surgery that involves the prostate, bladder, or colon may cut the nerves involved in the erection process, causing impotence.

Vascular Disease

Vascular disease, which affects the flow of blood through arteries and veins, is a major cause of impotence, especially in older men. Poor blood flow to the penis increases the time it takes to achieve a full erection, and decreases the rigidity of the erect penis. Conditions associated with poor blood flow include high blood pressure, hardening of the arteries (arteriosclerosis), high choles-

Table 2: The Nervous System and Impotence

Certain disorders of the nervous system are associated with erectile dysfunction. Some of these are listed below, along with the percentage of patients with these conditions who are impotent.

Disorders of the Central Nervous System
- Parkinson's disease: 60%
- Multiple sclerosis: 70%
- Spinal cord injury or disease: 5%-80%, depending on location
- Others (epilepsy, trauma, tumor): unknown

Peripheral Neuropathy
- Diabetes: (35%-70%)
- Others (alcoholism, aging, AIDS, vitamin deficiencies): unknown

After Surgery
- Prostate surgery (through the urethra): 4%
- Prostate removal for cancer (entire prostate is removed via an incision): 40%-90%

After Trauma (often involves nerves and arteries)
- Pelvic fracture: 50%
- Bicycle injury: unknown

---

terol, diabetes, pelvic trauma, and radiation therapy in the pelvic area. Impotence can also result from venous leak, in which tissue atrophy or scarring occurs within the penis, resulting in blood escaping from the penis similar to how air escapes from a leaking balloon (Figure 3).

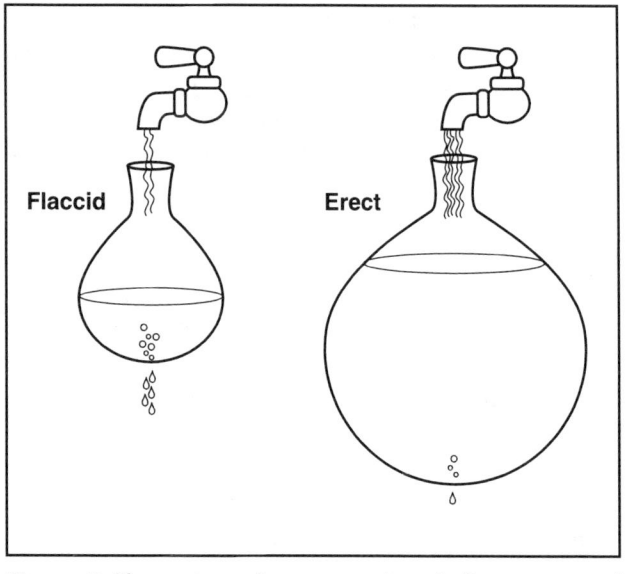

Figure 3: *The penis can be compared to a balloon connected to a faucet. In the flaccid penis, the inflow and outflow are minimal (left). During erection, the inflow is at its maximum, while the outflow is markedly reduced so that blood is retained in the erectile tissue to expand and lengthen the penis (right). If the outflow channels remain widely open, the balloon can not be filled; this is analogous to impotence caused by venous leak seen in many men.*

Diabetes

Diabetes is one of the most common causes of impotence. In fact, about 50% of all diabetic men experience impotence. Impotence caused by diabetes can be related to both nerve damage and poor blood flow. Diabetes is caused by a deficiency in insulin, a hormone that helps the body convert sugar (glucose) into energy. However, the hormone deficiency alone doesn't cause impotence. The damage to the nervous system, cardiovascular system and other major organs caused by diabetes can cause ED. Unfortunately, many men with diabetes are not aware that impotence is a potential complication of the disease.

Hormone Deficiency

Although doctors once believed that a low level of the male sex hormone testosterone caused impotence, it is now generally recognized that testosterone is not directly involved in the physical process of an erection. However, a low level of testosterone does decrease sexual desire, which ultimately affects the ability to achieve an erection. A dysfunction in the thyroid gland resulting in either too much thyroid hormone (hyperthyroidism), or too little (hypothyroidism), may contribute to erectile dysfunction.

In rare cases, a tumor in the pituitary gland of the brain can produce an excessive amount of a hormone called prolactin that can suppress the production of testosterone and thereby cause loss of sexual drive as well as erectile dysfunction.

Prescription Drugs

Impotence is a fairly common side effect of some prescription drugs. The mechanism of action is mostly unknown, and few well-controlled studies have examined how specific drugs affect sexual function. However, several classes of drugs are known to cause impotence in some men. They include antidepressants (taken for depression and anxiety) and some of the medications used to treat pain, high blood pressure, stomach ulcer, and prostate cancer. If you suspect that your ED is associated with taking a prescription drug, discuss it with your physician.

Alcohol: a two-edged sword in impotence

In Act II, Scene III of Shakespeare's *Macbeth*, a porter says to Macduff, "Drink (alcohol) is a great provoker of three things: nose-painting, sleep, and urine. It provokes, and unprovokes: it provokes the desire, but it takes away the performance." This is an elegant description of the pharmacologic effects of alcohol. In small amounts, alcohol is a central anxiolytic and thus decreases the normal cerebral inhibition and provokes desire; its vasodilatory effect also enhances penile erection. However, in large amounts, alcohol is a strong sedative-hypnotic. When a man can barely keep his eyes open, he is not likely to want to have sex.

You should never stop treatment, or change the dosage of a prescribed drug, without seeking medical advice.

Substance Abuse

Excessive use of alcohol, cigarettes, and illegal drugs often decreases sexual drive, and can seriously damage the blood vessels and nerves involved in achieving and maintaining a normal erection. Excessive tobacco use, in particular, can cause blockages in the penile artery and can heighten the effects of other risk factors for impotence, such as hypertension and cardiovascular disease. A study of nocturnal (overnight) erections in cigarette smokers showed that men who smoked more than 40 cigarettes a day had the weakest and shortest nocturnal erections.

Alcohol in small amounts improves sexual drive and erection because it dilates (widens) the blood vessels and suppresses anxiety. However, large amounts of alcohol can cause central sedation, decreased desire, and temporary ED (see *Alcohol: a two-edged sword in impotence*). Chronic alcoholism may also result in liver dysfunction, decreased testosterone levels, increased estrogen levels, and damage to peripheral nerves, including those in the penis.

Aging

Although impotence is not an inevitable consequence of aging, it does affect more older men than younger men. A number of studies have indicated a progressive decline in sexual function in 'healthy' older men. They may require a longer period of time to achieve an erection; the erect penis may be less swollen; the ejaculation may be smaller and less forceful; and it may take longer to recover from ejaculation sufficiently to re-engage in sexual intercourse. Other research has shown that the penis becomes less sensitive to touch as a man ages. These factors may all be involved in occasional ED, but, most often, chronic impotence can be traced to one of the physical conditions commonly associated with aging, coupled with the psychological implications associated with the disease or condition. This results in *impotence of mixed origin*.

One example of impotence of mixed origin is patients with severe lung disease, who often fear that sexual intercourse will aggravate their difficulty in breathing. Other examples are patients with angina, heart failure, or those who have suffered a heart attack, all of whom can become impotent from anxiety, depression, insufficient blood flow, or a combination of all three.

As you have learned, the penis is a specialized blood vessel controlled by your mind, nervous system, circulatory system, and hormone levels. Any condition that affects any of these functions can adversely affect penile erection. You should realize that occasional ED is nothing to worry about; however, if you're experiencing chronic impotence, you should not be reluctant to discuss it with your doctor. Thanks to many recent medical and pharmaceutical advances, most men who experience chronic ED can be successfully treated.

Chapter 2

Finding the Cause

Because erectile dysfunction (ED) often has an emotional component, the search for the cause begins with you. You can do a number of things before seeing your doctor to provide valuable information about the cause of your ED. By considering aspects of your life that might affect your ability to achieve an erection, you may find the cause and be able to correct the situation without consulting your doctor. At the very least, you may obtain important information that can help your doctor make an accurate diagnosis. Answering the following questions can provide important clues to the cause of your impotence:

- Have you started taking a new prescription or over-the counter-medication? If so, check with your doctor or pharmacist to see if impotence is a possible side effect of that particular drug. *Remember: Never stop taking a prescription medication, or alter the dosage, without discussing it with your doctor.*
- Do you have diabetes, high blood pressure, or high cholesterol? These are common causes of impotence.
- Have you had any recent physical injuries involving your back, spine, or genitals?
- Are factors in your life creating distractions that can make it difficult to achieve or maintain an erection, such as exceptional stress at work, tension in your re-

lationship with your partner, a lack of privacy for lovemaking, or a recent loss?

- Are you allowing enough time for foreplay? Men over age 50 often take longer than younger men to become sexually aroused. They may also require more direct stimulation by their partner.
- Are you drinking or smoking excessively?
- Are you able to have an erection at other times—through masturbation or on awakening? If you regularly awaken during the night or in the morning with a full erection, your ED may be related to stress or an emotional problem.

If you feel that your ED has a psychological or emotional component, you may want to try some self-care before consulting your physician. Erection problems often can be resolved by coping with stress through exercise and other tension-relieving activities; by making sure you get enough rest; by eating a healthy, well-balanced diet; and by avoiding alcohol and smoking. It's also important to take a relaxed approach to lovemaking. Allow yourself and your partner sufficient time and privacy to become fully aroused, before attempting intercourse. Allow more time for foreplay, and let your partner know that you would like more stroking. Making these adjustments will certainly not diminish sexual pleasure for you or your partner. In fact, they are more likely to enhance the experience for both of you.

When to See a Doctor

Erectile dysfunction can affect men at any age. If you experience an occasional incidence of impotence, you should not view it as a signal that your sex life is about to end. Dwelling on it and anticipating that it will happen

The difficulty in isolating the cause of impotence

Because many older men are lonely, are somewhat depressed, and take multiple medications for a number of diseases, it is difficult to determine whether the impotence is a side effect of a particular drug or of the interaction of several drugs, the manifestation of the underlying diseases, or results from a combination of the above. For example, β-blockers may enhance α-adrenoceptor function, and thus may make the erectile smooth muscles and arterioles more difficult to relax. Additionally, in a patient with a stenotic penile artery from chronic hypertension, a high systolic pressure (eg, 180 mm Hg) may be required to maintain cavernous arterial pressure (eg, 120 mm Hg) and a solid erection (eg, 90 mm Hg of intracavernous pressure). Once the antihypertensives take effect and the blood pressure is normalized (120 mm Hg), the pressure in the cavernous artery also drops (eg, to 80 mm Hg), resulting in a partial erection (eg, 60 mm Hg intracavernous pressure). This differential pressure phenomenon may explain the paradox that almost all the antihypertensive drugs have been reported to cause impotence.

again may actually turn into the proverbial 'self-fulfilling prophecy.' It's best to put it behind you and assume that your next sexual encounter will be successful.

If you think a medication may be responsible for your ED (see *The difficulty in isolating the cause of impotence*), if you find that you are unable to have an erection at all, or if your episodes of impotence persist despite your attempts at self-care, it may be time to see a doctor. Several types of doctors treat ED:

- family practitioners
- urologists
- internists
- endocrinologists
- psychiatrists
- psychologists

It's best to start with your family doctor, or primary care physician—who is probably a family practitioner or an internist—because he or she already knows your medical history and your current state of health. Your doctor will help determine the cause of your impotence, and assist you in selecting an appropriate treatment. If your family doctor prefers not to treat you, he or she may refer you to a *urologist*, who specializes in treating conditions related to the genitourinary system. If your doctor finds evidence of a hormone deficiency, he or she may prescribe hormone replacement therapy for you, or refer you to an *endocrinologist* for further testing and treatment. If your doctor is unable to find a physical cause for your impotence, or feels that your emotions are a contributing factor, he or she may want you to consult with a *psychiatrist* or a *psychologist*. If you are not comfortable with your current doctor, or don't have one, refer to Chapter 6 for advice on finding a doctor.

An important word of caution: If a doctor offers a treatment option without thoroughly evaluating your medical and sexual history and conducting a basic physical examination, it would be wise to see another doctor. A reputable physician will not prescribe treat-

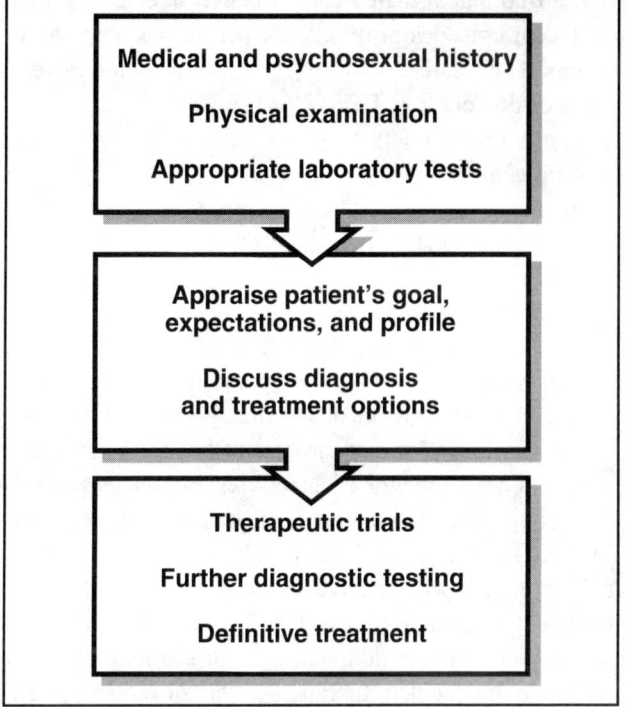

Figure 1: *Patient's goal-directed approach to diagnosis and treatment of erectile dysfunction.*

ment without taking a medical history and conducting a physical examination.

Making the Diagnosis

Physicians differ in the way they practice medicine, but a basic work-up generally includes a medical history, including the psychological and sexual aspects; a physical examination; and appropriate laboratory testing (Figure 1).

Medical History

If you have been seeing a doctor on a regular basis, he or she should have your medical history, but the information will need to be updated. The doctor will ask you questions about recent physical ailments; about your use of prescription, over-the-counter, or illegal drugs; and about your alcohol consumption and smoking habits. Because ED is associated with many common medical conditions and medications, your accurate responses to these questions can provide important clues to the cause of your ED. For example, if you have a long history of diabetes, there's a strong possibility that your impotence is related to vascular disease or neuropathy, which are common complications of diabetes. Also, if you recently began taking a new medication to control high blood pressure, that could provide an important clue.

The doctor will also ask questions about your levels of stress and fatigue, as well as detailed questions about your sex life and your relationship with your partner. Some of these questions may seem too personal and embarrassing, but your doctor needs to know about your emotional health and your sexual functioning to correctly diagnose and treat your impotence. You should try to answer all questions as accurately, honestly, and candidly as possible. Your sexual history provides important information that helps the doctor decide what further evaluation is needed. One of the most important questions your doctor will ask is: "Do you wake up in the morning with a full, firm erection?" If you always wake up with an erection, it is unlikely that your impotence is caused by a physical problem. If you never wake up with a firm erection, then a physical problem with your blood flow or your nerves may be the cause.

The effects of testosterone

Many of my patients have been given testosterone preparations by their family physician or urologist before coming to see me. In one major study, testosterone had virtually no association with impotence. However, millions of dollars are spent every year because of the false belief that testosterone boosts sexual drive and, therefore, improves potency. Because of the high incidence of prostate cancer in older men, the indiscriminate prescription of testosterone may speed the growth of many microscopic prostate cancers and pose a real threat to a patient's well-being. Before giving testosterone to any man over 45 years old, a detailed prostate examination (including prostate-specific antigen test and, if necessary, prostate ultrasound and biopsy) is strongly recommended.

The Physical Examination

A thorough physical examination, with special attention to your genitals, can provide important information and, occasionally, reveal an obvious cause of ED. For example, small, soft, shriveled testicles or abnormal secondary sex characteristics, such as enlarged breasts or an abnormal hair pattern, suggest a hormonal problem. The doctor will also carefully check the nerves in the genital area. If the penis does not respond as expected when touched in a certain way, impotence may be attributed to a problem in the nervous system. Examination of the genitals may also reveal abnormalities that could interfere with effective treatment, such as Peyronie's disease, a curvature of the penis caused by plaque formation. Peyronie's disease is addressed further in Chapter 5.

The physical examination may also offer other, less obvious clues to the cause of ED. For example, the presence of high blood pressure, an irregular heartbeat, or an *abdominal aneurysm*—a ballooning of the aorta, which is the main blood vessel leading to the heart—might indicate a circulatory problem that can affect your ability to achieve and maintain an erection.

Laboratory Tests

A number of fairly routine laboratory tests can identify treatable conditions or previously undetected medical illnesses that can contribute to ED. A basic laboratory evaluation generally includes a complete blood count, a lipid profile to determine your cholesterol level, a blood sugar test, a urinalysis, kidney and liver function tests, and a check of your morning testosterone level (see *The effects of testosterone*).

Additional Testing

Depending on what your doctor finds, or doesn't find, after reviewing your medical history, physical examination and laboratory tests, he or she may recommend monitoring erections during sleep, called *nocturnal penile tumescence* (NPT). This test can help distinguish between psychological and physical causes of impotence. If erections do not occur during sleep, the cause of impotence is likely to be physical. If they do occur, then the cause is more likely psychological. NPT is not an invasive test, but many impotence specialists question its clinical usefulness. Anxiety and depression can sometimes influence an individual's dreams, and negatively affect spontaneous nocturnal erections. Also, some patients with vascular problems that cause them to lose their erection during pelvic thrusts may experience normal nocturnal erections.

A number of other tests can further pinpoint the exact cause of ED. However, in most cases, your doctor will discuss treatment options with you based on the results of the medical history, physical examination, and basic laboratory tests. Your doctor's decision to conduct further, often more invasive tests, would be based on the treatment option you choose and your ultimate goal in seeking treatment.

Chapter 3

Treatment Options

Thanks to recent medical advances, a number of treatments are available for erectile dysfunction (ED). Your doctor will recommend one based on several factors, including your general health, the cause and severity of your impotence, the preferences of both you and your partner, and cost. Physicians generally agree that the approach to treatment should begin with the least invasive method, moving on to the most invasive procedure only if all other treatments fail. However, before deciding to pursue treatment of any kind, you need to decide if you really want to follow through. Your responses to these questions may help you make this decision:

- How motivated are you to resume normal sexual activity?
- How much support do you have from your partner?
- How willing are you to learn and use new techniques?

Men and women who go without sexual activity for a long time often fall out of the habit of having sex, and may not particularly miss it. The likelihood of success is not good if you are considering treatment just because you're wondering whether it will work. Your chances for success are much greater if you and your partner are eager to resume regular sexual activity.

Although some men prefer to deal with their ED without involving their partner, most doctors agree that couples who work together to seek treatment gain the most benefit. Ideally, this involvement should begin with the first visit to your doctor, because your partner often can provide valuable information that can help the doctor find the cause and recommend treatment. At the very least, your partner should be consulted before making a final decision about treatment. Here are some things to consider:

- Is your partner as eager as you are to become sexually active again?
- Is your partner willing to help you make treatment decisions?
- Will your partner have sex with you using the selected treatment?

Many treatments for ED require a man to take some physical action to achieve an erection. Some of them require time and effort to learn. If you are looking for a quick and easy solution, or are resistant to finding new ways to achieve an erection, you will probably not be successful with some of the available treatments.

Nonmedical Treatment

Lifestyle or Medication Changes

If your doctor believes that your ED is related to excessive alcohol consumption, smoking, or drug abuse, the obvious solution is to make the appropriate lifestyle changes. Certain classes of medication are associated with ED. If your doctor suspects your erectile dysfunction is related to a recently prescribed medication, he or she may decide to change your medication, reduce the dosage, or eliminate it completely if doing so will not adversely affect your health. In patients with generalized vascular disease, which can affect the flow of blood to the penis as well as to other parts of the body, eliminating smoking, reducing fatty food intake, and starting regular exercise can improve erectile function. Drinking excessive amounts of alcohol (hard liquor or more than a bottle of wine a day) may increase hormone production that suppresses your sexual function or damages nerves in the penis. Consider reducing your alcohol intake to the equivalent of 1 glass of wine a day, which can actually reduce the chances of developing these problems. Your doctor may also recommend regular exercise or changes in diet that can improve your blood flow. If your hobby is long-distance bicycle riding, your doctor may suggest you find a new hobby, or change your bicycle seat. That's because frequent, extended periods of bicycling can cause repeated minor trauma to blood vessels or nerves to the penis.

Psychosexual Therapy

If your doctor finds that your ED has a psychological cause, you may be referred to a psychiatrist, psychologist, or sex therapist for treatment. In fact, even if your doctor finds a physical cause for your ED, he or she may recommend counseling to help relieve anxiety and remove unrealistic expectations associated with medical or surgical therapy. Because emotional factors are ultimately involved in almost all cases of ED, many doctors believe that some form of psychosexual counseling should be part of the treatment for many patients suffering from ED.

Three types of psychotherapy are commonly used to treat sexual dysfunction. *Individual psychoanalytic therapy* is based on the theory that sexual dysfunction represents an underlying subconscious conflict. If the patient's erectile problems are associated with an emotional response that no longer applies to him, he can learn to create a new image of himself that will break through certain emotional barriers and cure his erectile problems. The drawback of this treatment is that it requires prolonged, intense therapy. Also, no data show the long-term success of this kind of therapy.

Symptom-oriented therapy often includes the patient's sexual partner. This therapy primarily involves explaining the cause of the dysfunction, providing sexual information, and offering reassurance, encouragement, and advice.

Cognitive-behavioral therapy also includes the patient's sexual partner. The goal is to make couples trust each other more and help them become more comfortable with sex. This type of therapy often focuses on lessening the fear of failure by directing attention to sensual and sexual pleasure. Cognitive-behavioral treatment works best when the doctor takes the time to learn as much as possible about the patient to determine an individualized approach for every couple. Education is very important in this method of treatment. Couples must tell each other what arouses them. Sometimes, men and women don't fully understand how to arouse their partners, and need to learn basic arousal skills. Generally, the more one partner learns about the other's body, the more they both learn how to give and receive sensual pleasure. Sexual partners often develop routines that no longer work after several years. These couples need to communicate and try new things to shift their focus from performance to pleasure.

Sex Therapy

In the 1970s, well-known sex therapists Masters and Johnson developed a sex therapy program designed to separate sexuality from performance anxiety, inhibition,

Table 1: Unfavorable Conditions for Psychosexual Therapy

Some circumstances and conditions make successful sex therapy more difficult and unlikely. These include:

- Uncooperative patient or sexual partner
- Low sex drive
- Psychosis or major mood disorder
- Significant interpersonal problems with sexual partner
- Failure of previous psychosexual therapy

---

and guilt. It involves a series of exercises that teach men and women to enjoy their own and their partner's body, using all their senses, in a relaxed and erotic way. During the initial exercises, couples are advised to abstain from intercourse. As therapy progresses, stimulation of sexual organs is encouraged and, when erection returns, the couple can progress to intercourse. The success rate of this type of sex therapy ranges from 35% to 80%, and is related to the type and severity of ED.

However, some conditions and circumstances make sex therapy impractical (Table 1).

Hormonal Therapy

A severe deficiency of testosterone—also called *hypogonadism*—can cause impotence. However, only about 4% of the male population has this problem and can benefit from treatment, which usually involves giving testosterone either through a skin patch or by injection in the arm or buttocks to raise the hormone to acceptable levels.

Recently, the idea of 'male menopause,' also referred to as andropause, has received a good deal of publicity in the popular press, but many doctors are skeptical that it exists. If male menopause does exist, it involves a gradual decline of hormone levels and body function, and is quite different from female menopause. Symptoms of male menopause may include hot flashes, mood swings, insomnia (difficulty sleeping), depression, irritability, decreased sexual desire, impotence, weakness, lethargy (listlessness or drowsiness), loss of lean body mass, and decreased bone mass. The relationship of these symptoms to declining levels of male hormones is controversial, and the benefit of hormone replacement therapy (HRT) in relieving them is still unproven.

HRT is effective in men who have a medically confirmed testosterone deficiency; however, sadly, millions of dollars are spent every year because of the false belief that testosterone boosts sexual drive and, therefore, improves potency. The side effects of testosterone replacement therapy can be serious, and the indiscriminate prescribing of testosterone may speed the growth of many microscopic prostate cancers. HRT should be avoided by patients with a history of liver disease, heart disease, kidney problems, urinary problems, or prostate cancer. If your doctor recommends testosterone replacement therapy without conducting the appropriate laboratory tests, you should seek another opinion before proceeding with treatment.

Drug Therapy
Viagra®

Viagra® is the first oral medication designed specifically to treat impotence. Known generically as sildenafil citrate, Viagra® works by blocking an enzyme (PDE5), found in the penis, that breaks down a chemical (cyclic GMP), which is produced during sexual stimulation. The longer GMP remains available, the greater the chance of achieving and maintaining an erection. Unlike other drugs commonly used to treat impotence, which are addressed later in this chapter, Viagra® does not cause an erection unless the man is sexually stimulated.

Viagra® was tested on several thousand men with mild, moderate, or complete erectile dysfunction. These men had a broad range of conditions associated with ED, including high blood pressure, high cholesterol, diabetes, and prostate surgery. Viagra® was effective in 50% to 80% of the men who participated in 21 clinical trials. Men with diabetes and those with a history of radical prostate surgery showed less improvement than other groups. No evidence suggests that Viagra® enhances the sexual performance of healthy men.

Available by prescription in 25-mg, 50-mg, and 100-mg strengths, Viagra® is taken on an as-needed basis, 1 hour before sexual activity, but not more than once a day. Although the cost varies, it generally runs between $8 and $10 a pill. The most common side effects associated with Viagra® are headache, flushing, indigestion, stuffy nose, and diarrhea. In addition, about 3% of patients participating in the clinical trials reported temporary changes in their vision, including sensitivity to light and seeing a bluish tinge. Men who use nitroglycerin, either in a patch or as a pill under the tongue, or other heart medicines containing nitrates should not take Viagra® because combining the two may lower blood pressure to life-threatening levels (Table 2). No studies have been conducted to test the safety

Table 2: Recommendations for Sildenafil and the Cardiac Patient

Contraindicated in:
- Patients taking long-acting or short-acting nitrate drugs

Caution should be exercised in patients:
- with stable coronary disease (pre-sildenafil treadmill test may be indicated to assess the risk of cardiac ischemia during sexual intercourse)
- with congestive heart failure who have borderline low blood pressure and low volume status
- who are on a complicated, multidrug, antihypertension therapy regimen
- who are on other medications or have conditions that can prolong the duration of action of sildenafil

---

and effectiveness of Viagra® when combined with other treatments for impotence or other prescription medications. Therefore, you should tell your doctor about all the medications you are taking, including over-the-counter drugs.

The FDA approval of Viagra® in March 1998 created tremendous excitement in the medical community and in the general public. The good news is that it has drawn much-needed attention to a problem that has been undertreated, primarily because men have felt uncomfortable discussing it with their doctors. Before Viagra®, many men wouldn't even admit they had ED. Now, men from all walks of life, including former Senator Robert Dole, are willing to discuss it on national television.

The bad news is a real danger of misuse and overuse, partly because of the level of media attention Viagra® has received. During the first month of availability, demand for Viagra® was unprecedented. According to one newspaper report, as many as 40,000 people a day were seeking prescriptions. One concern is that healthy men are seeking to take Viagra® as a way to enhance their sexual performance and pleasure. Also, physicians are concerned that some men will experiment with higher-than-recommended doses. Viagra® does not work for everyone suffering from ED, and *no evidence suggests that Viagra® enhances the performance of healthy potent men*. In addition, side effects associated with Viagra® could have potentially serious consequences for some men.

Although the changes in retinal function were temporary in men who took the recommended dose, and occurred in only 3% of those participating in the clinical trials, people with eye conditions affecting the retina, such as macular degeneration or retinitis pigmentosa, should be cautious about using Viagra®.

If you are not under the regular care of a physician, or have never before consulted your doctor about your ED, you should have a complete medical history and physical examination to determine the cause of your impotence before taking Viagra®. If your doctor offers to prescribe Viagra® without thoroughly discussing your medical and sexual history and conducting a basic physical examination, it would be wise to consult another doctor.

Injectable Drugs

Until very recently, the most effective drug therapy for treating impotence was injecting one of three different drugs, or a combination, directly into the side of the penis. These drugs create an erection by relaxing the smooth muscles and widening the blood vessels in the penis. Although this method, known as *intracavernous injection*, is very effective in treating most types of impotence, it has a number of drawbacks. Many men are squeamish about injecting themselves; spontaneity is lacking; and the drugs may cause undesirable side effects, including a persistent erection (priapism) lasting for hours or days and scarring. For more information about priapism, see Chapter 5.

Three drugs are used for intracavernous injection. Papaverine was the first drug to be used, and is the least expensive. The other two are phentolamine and alprostadil, which is a synthetic version of prostaglandin E_1, a substance naturally produced by the body. Many doctors combine the three drugs to improve drug potency and reduce the incidence of pain.

Papaverine is generally very effective in treating impotence that is psychologically or neurologically based. Its major advantages are its low cost and stability at room temperature. The primary disadvantages are the higher incidences of scarring.

Phentolamine, when used alone, is clinically less effective. However, it has a low incidence of side effects such as priapism and scarring. The most common side effects associated with phentolamine are low blood pressure, rapid heartbeat, nasal congestion, and stomach upset.

Alprostadil was the first treatment approved by the FDA specifically for impotence. Marketed as Caverject® or Edex® it has a higher response rate than papaverine and a lower incidence of priapism and scarring, but a much higher incidence of painful erection (Table 3).

Table 3: Pros and Cons of Common Intracavernous Agents

After consultation with you, your doctor may prescribe one of these injectable drugs or drug combinations:

Drug	Advantages	Disadvantages/ Side Effects
Papaverine	Low cost Stable at room temperature	Fibrosis (scarring), priapism (persistent, painful erection).
Papaverine + phentolamine	More potent than papaverine alone	Fibrosis, priapism Requires refrigeration
Alprostadil	Priapism rare	Pain more common
Papaverine + phentolamine + alprostadil	Most potent	Requires refrigeration Fibrosis, priapism

The most frequent side effects of alprostadil are pain at the site of injection or during erection, slight bruising, and priapism.

Men who choose intracavernous injections to treat their ED must learn to inject either side of the penis with the appropriate amount of drug, as determined by their physician (usually less than 1 cc). They then must apply hand pressure for 5 minutes to prevent bleeding. Erections usually occur in 5 to 10 minutes, last for 30 minutes or so, and become more rigid if sexual stimulation occurs. Intracavernous injection therapy should not be used in patients with schizophrenia or other severe psychiatric disorders, active veneral disease, or conditions associated

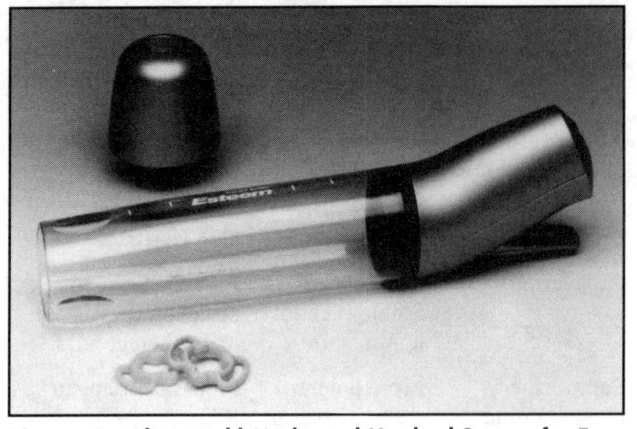

Figure 1: *Alprostadil Medicated Urethral System for Erection (MUSE®).*

with priapism such as sickle cell anemia, leukemia, or bone marrow tumors. In patients with poor manual dexterity or poor eyesight, the sexual partner can be instructed to perform the injection. Cost per injection ranges from $5 to $25. Table 3 lists the pros and cons of the common intercavernous agents.

Intraurethral Suppository

In 1996, the FDA approved a new delivery method for alprostadil. Marketed under the trade name MUSE® (medicated urethral system for erection), it involves depositing a tiny suppository, about the size of a grain of rice, into the urethra. After urination, a small applicator is inserted about 1 inch into the opening at the tip of the penis. Gently pushing a button located at the top of the applicator (Figure 1) deposits the suppository into the urethra where it is absorbed, causing rapid inflow of blood and penile erection.

Although this treatment doesn't involve needles, some men may still find the method painful or uncomfortable. Because it is an indirect approach, men are advised to stand up for 10 minutes after application to decrease the chances of the suppository being absorbed into the body. To help sustain the erection, a rubber band may need to be placed around the base of the penis. An adjustable constriction device (Actis®) is available for this purpose. Side effects associated with intraurethral therapy include minor bleeding in the urethra, mild to moderate pain or a slight burning sensation, and dizziness. Patients must receive thorough instructions from a physician or nurse to ensure safe and effective use of this method. The cost is about $25 per use.

Yohimbine

Although there is controversy about its effectiveness, yohimbine, a natural aphrodisiac derived from the bark of the yohimb tree, has been used for years to treat men with erectile dysfunction. Yohimbine is available in different formulations either over the counter or by prescription (Yocon®, Yohimex™, Aphrodyne®). Doctors sometimes prescribe it when they suspect a psychological problem but can't confirm it. Yohimbine is usually taken in tablet form 3 times a day. Side effects may include headaches, sweaty palms, dizziness, and nausea. Men with ulcers or hypertension should not take yohimbine.

An analysis of seven randomized, double-blind trials that compared yohimbine and a placebo in treating ED showed a response rate of 34% to 73% with yohimbine, and from 4% to 45% with placebo. The trials included men with both physical and emotional impotence, and

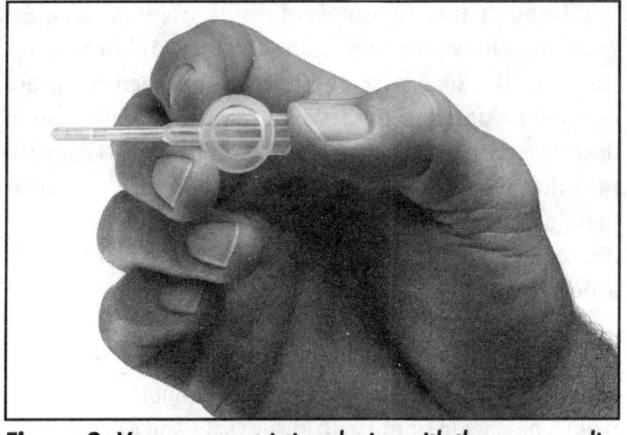

Figure 2: *Vacuum constriction device with the pump, cylinder, and constriction band. (Courtesy of Osbon-Imagyn).*

involved doses from 5 to 10 mg given 3 times a day. In each study, yohimbine was superior to placebo, although the difference wasn't statistically significant in some of the trials. Many doctors are unconvinced that yohimbine is an effective treatment for ED, particularly if there is a physical cause.

External Vacuum Therapy

The vacuum constriction device is an effective and safe treatment for ED, when used properly, and is one of the least costly treatment options ($150 to $450). It works by creating a partial vacuum around the penis, which draws blood into the penis, creating an erection. The typical vacuum device (Figure 2) has three components: a hollow plastic tube, into which the penis is placed; a pump, either manual or battery operated, that draws air out of the cylinder; and a rubber ring, which is placed at the base of the penis after the cylinder is removed to maintain the erection by preventing blood from draining out of the penis.

To use a vacuum constriction device such as Esteem® (Timm Medical), you stretch the rubber ring (tension ring) over the end of the plastic cylinder and then insert your penis into that end. Holding the device firmly against your body to form an air seal, you use the pump to remove air from inside the cylinder. While your penis is still under vacuum pressure, you push the tension ring from the cylinder on to the base of the penis to sustain the erection. The cylinder is removed and set aside. This procedure takes about 2 minutes. To avoid injury to your penis, the tension ring should not be left in place for more than 30 minutes.

The erection produced by a vacuum device is different from a natural erection or one produced by intracavernous injection. The base of the penis may be limp, the penile skin may be cold and dusky, and ejaculation may be trapped by the tension ring, which may be uncomfortable or even painful. Despite these differences, many patients find that the device produces an erection that is close to normal, and rigid enough for successful intercourse. Studies have shown that many men who use the vacuum device are satisfied with the quality of the erection; partner satisfaction is also high. Complications include penile pain and numbness, difficult ejaculation, bruising, the appearance of reddish pinpoint-size dots on the surface of the penis, pain or swelling after the device is used, and temperature drop in the penis caused by the tension ring. Patients taking aspirin or other drugs to thin the blood should exercise caution when using the vacuum device. It is not recommended in patients with sickle cell anemia or leukemia.

Table 4: Indications and Contraindications to Vacuum Constriction Device Therapy

Certain conditions rule out the safe use of the vacuum device. You should not attempt this form of therapy if you:

- have sickle cell disease
- are taking anticoagulation therapy (eg, heparin, Coumadin®)
- have a bleeding disorder
- have a severe penile deformity
- have recurrent priapism
- have an active sexually transmitted or other infectious disease

Vacuum constriction devices are particularly useful, however, in certain circumstances, including:

- after radical prostatectomy (helps initiate and maintain erection, and prevents shortening of the penis).
- after penile surgery (prevents shortening of the penis).
- after removal of a penile prosthesis (prevents shortening of the penis).
- after venous grafting (a procedure for Peyronie's disease, addressed in Chapter 5; the device stretches the graft, causing the tissue to expand).

The vacuum device helps prevent the penis from shortening when applied for 30 minutes a day, without using the constriction band.

Table 5: Vacuum Constriction Devices

Company	Device
Timm Medical	ErecAid®, Esteem®
Post-T-Vac	Post-T-Vac® system
Mentor	Response® system
Vetco	VET® system
Encore	VTU® system

Table 4 lists the indications and contraindications to vacuum constriction device therapy.

Understandably, the vacuum device is more acceptable to older men in a steady relationship than it is to young, single men in search of a partner. Although many of these devices are available without a prescription and can be used by any patient with ED, you should see your doctor for a medical examination, including a complete history, physical examination, and appropriate laboratory tests. This will rule out an easily correctable cause of the impotence. These devices can be difficult to use, especially for patients with poor manual dexterity, and training in the correct use is important to avoid damaging the penis. Including the sexual partner in training can help to establish a mutually satisfying level of sexual activity.

Several vacuum constriction devices have been approved for medical use by the FDA (Table 5). Similar devices are available from sex shops, at a lower cost, but it is best to consult with your physician before using them. A word of warning: do not try to use your household vacuum cleaner. The pressure is much too high, and you could seriously injure your penis.

Table 6: Penile Prosthesis: Indications and Contraindications

A penile prosthesis may be viable for certain patients:
- those who fail or will not tolerate less invasive therapies (such as vacuum constriction devices or penile injection)

A penile prosthesis is not warranted for patients:
- who have a temporary or reversible form of impotence
- who have unrealistic expectations
- who are convicted sex offenders
- with an active sexually transmitted or other infectious disease

---

Vascular Surgery

There are two types of vascular surgery as a treatment for ED: (1) arterial bypass to improve blood flow to the penis, and (2) venous surgery to reduce the outflow from the penis (reduce or stop the leak). Bypass surgery is quite successful in young men whose impotence is the result of localized blockage of the penile artery after injury to the pelvis or the penis. Bypass surgery is not useful in patients with generalized hardening of the arteries (atherosclerosis).

Similarly, venous surgery has been reasonably successful in young patients suffering from life-long impotence or from impotence from penile injury. However, venous surgery is not effective in older men with atrophy of the penile erectile tissues.

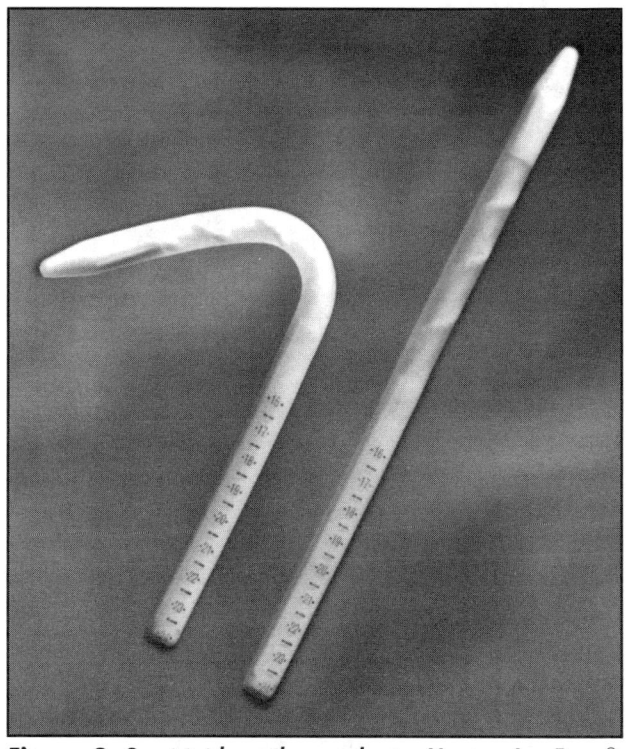

Figure 3: *Semirigid penile prosthesis, Mentor Acu-Form®. (Courtesy of Mentor, Inc.)*

Penile Prostheses

Implanted devices, known as prostheses, are highly successful in restoring erection in many men with ED. However, because it requires surgery, it is considered a last resort. Doctors generally do not recommend a penile prosthesis until patients have tried the less invasive alternative therapies. Table 6 lists the indications and contraindications of penile prosthesis therapy. If

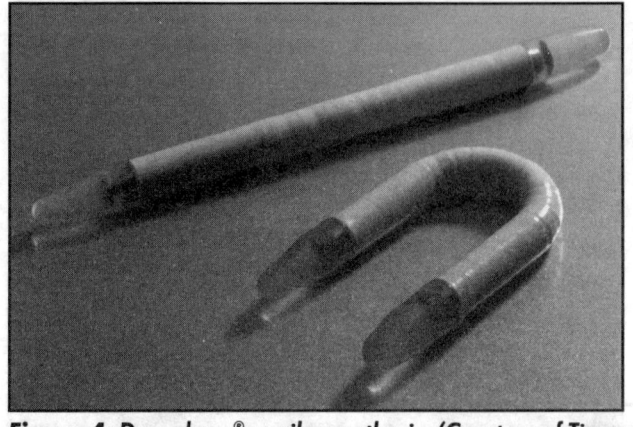

Figure 4: Duraphase® penile prosthesis. (Courtesy of Timm Medical.)

other treatments fail or patients find them unsatisfactory, a prosthesis may be an appropriate alternative. The three general types of penile prostheses are semirigid (malleable), mechanical, and inflatable devices (Figures 3-5 and Table 7).

Malleable implants usually consist of silicone rubber rods that are inserted in the corpora cavernosa. The position of the penis can be adjusted to simulate an erection, but the width and length of the penis do not change. The *mechanical implant* is also made of silicone rubber, but it contains interlocking rings in a rod column that provides rigidity when the rings are lined up and flaccidity when the penis is bent.

Inflatable implants are available in 1-piece, 2-piece, and 3-piece units. The 1-piece unit consists of two cylinders that are surgically inserted inside the penis, which can be expanded using pressurized fluid, located in a fluid reservoir, from a pump located at the tip of the cylinders.

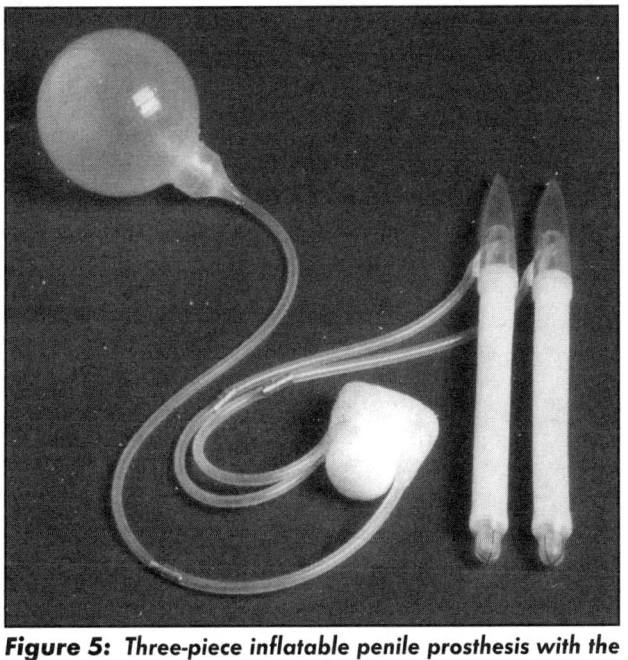

Figure 5: *Three-piece inflatable penile prosthesis with the reservoir implanted in the prevesical area, cylinders within the corpora cavernosa, and pump in the scrotal sac. (Courtesy of American Medical Systems, Inc.)*

The 2-piece unit consists of the two cylinders attached to a pump-reservoir that is surgically placed in the scrotum (the pouch containing the testes and related organs). The 3-piece device consists of two cylinders, a scrotal pump, and a fluid reservoir that is implanted above the pubic arch. Pressing on the pump expands the cylinders creating an erection. Inflatable implants can somewhat expand the length and width of the penis. When the cylinders are not inflated, the penis is in a more natural state than it is with the malleable devices.

Table 7: Types of Penile Prosthesis

Type	Prosthesis	Vendor
Malleable	Accuform	Mentor
	600	AMS
	600M	AMS
Mechanical	Duraphase II	Timm Medical
Inflatable		
1-piece	Dynaflex	AMS
2-piece	Ambicor	AMS
	Mark II	Mentor
3-piece	inflatable (3 connectors)	Mentor
	Alpha-1 (1 connector)	Mentor
	700CX	AMS
	700CXM	AMS
	700 Ultrex (3 connectors)	AMS
	700 Ultrex Plus (1 connector)	AMS

AMS=American Medical Systems

Although all the available prostheses help patients achieve a successful erection, some patients do better with one device than with another. For example, men with impaired manual dexterity will do better with malleable or mechanical devices than with inflatable devices. On the other hand, for men with bladder cancer or any condition requiring frequent cystoscopy (visualization of the urinary tract) or procedures performed through the urethra, an inflatable device would be better.

Malleable devices generally last longer than the inflatable ones. The failure rate for penile prostheses is

5% to 15% in the first 5 years. Most devices will fail in 10 to 15 years and will need to be replaced. Potential complications include mechanical failures, cylinder leaks, tubing leaks, infection, perforation, persistent pain, and self-inflation.

Chapter 4

Making a Choice

The desire to take medicine is perhaps the greatest feature that distinguishes men from animals.
— Sir William Osler

The simple, inexpensive, reversible treatments for erectile dysfunction (ED) should generally be tried first. Now that an oral medication (Viagra®) is available, this would seem to be the obvious first solution. It is a simple, reversible treatment that is less expensive than some of the other options. However, some unpleasant side effects are associated with its use, its long-term safety has not yet been established, and it can be relatively expensive, depending on how frequently you have sexual relations. Also, it may not work for you. In a newspaper article that appeared shortly after Viagra® became available, one man reported spending $275 for 30 pills only to find that it didn't work for him, even after he increased the dose. A number of factors must be considered before making a final decision about treatment.

- If you have a spouse or regular sexual partner, it's important to consider her opinion. Does she find one treatment more acceptable than the others? It would be wise to ask her to go to the doctor with you so that she is fully aware of the advantages and disadvantages of each option.

- Consider how often you engage in sexual activity. Select a therapy that is consistent with how often it will be used. Men who select injection therapy often switch to another treatment after a few months if they frequently engage in sexual activity, because repeated needle punctures may cause scar tissue to build up in the penis.
- Be sure to ask your doctor about any compromises in lifestyle you may have to make. For example, a malleable implant may cause a permanently erect penis, something to consider when dressing for the beach.

Financial considerations are also important. What is the cost of the treatment to you? How much, if anything, will health insurance cover? Is it primarily a one-time expense (vacuum constriction devices and prostheses), or an ongoing expense (prescription drugs)? What are the guarantees of the treatment you select? What are the odds of having to repeat costly, and risky, surgeries (prostheses)?

Two of the most important things to consider are the safety and effectiveness of the treatment. Have clinical studies been performed to analyze the treatment? Is the treatment backed by a reputable provider, with liability insurance?

Don't hesitate to discuss all your concerns with your doctor. With the wide range of treatment options available, the chances are excellent that you and your partner can find something that works for both of you. The various pros and cons of treatment options are outlined in Table 1.

Table 1: Treatment options for erectile dysfunction

Each therapy for erectile dysfunction has advantages and disadvantages, as listed below:

Nonsurgical Treatment	Advantages
Counseling/sex therapy	• No surgery or drugs • Leads to understanding • Improves communication
Hormone replacement therapy	• Nonsurgical • May improve libido
Oral therapy: Viagra®	• Safe • Relative efficacy • Nonsurgical
Transurethral therapy: Muse®	• Local therapy • Few systemic side effects
Vacuum constriction device therapy	• Can be used as often as desired • Success rate about 60%
Penile injection therapy	• Highly effective (up to 90%) • Few systemic side effects

Surgical Treatment	Advantages
Penile implant surgery	• High patient/partner satisfaction
Vascular surgery	• Curative

Disadvantages	Cost
• Many require many sessions • Success rates vary	$50-$150 per session
• Effective only in patients with very low testosterone deficiency. May stimulate growth of prostate tissue or cause liver damage	$25-$35/mo, more if skin patch is used
• Cardiovascular issues 1-hour wait	$10/dose
• Moderate success rate (43% -60% with Actis®) • Penile pain	$25/dose
• May cause mild bruising, pain, or numbness	$150-$500
• Requires injection • Priapism or fibrosis may occur • Penile pain	$5-$25/dose

Disadvantages

• Requires surgical procedure • Risk of infection, device malfunction • Alters internal structure of penis and may prevent other treatment	$8,000-$15,000
• Poor results in older men with generalized disease • Requires anesthesia and surgery	$10,000-$15,000

Chapter 5

Other Conditions That May Cause Erectile Dysfunction

In rare cases, erectile dysfunction (ED) can be attributed to other, more complex causes than those mentioned in earlier chapters. This chapter addresses some of these conditions.

Priapism

Priapism is a persistent, often painful erection of the penis that is not accompanied by sexual stimulation or desire. It occurs when blood becomes trapped in the penis, causing it to become engorged. Without circulation, the blood becomes stagnant and loses oxygen. Although rare, priapism, which gets its name from Priapus, the Greek god of fertility, is a serious condition that needs immediate attention.

Many conditions can cause priapism, including the penile injections used to treat impotence. This is most likely to occur when a man decides to increase the dose of medication without consulting his doctor. Some other common causes of priapism are:

- diseases of the blood, such as sickle cell anemia and leukemia

- prolonged sexual activity
- injury to the spine or the penis
- infections of the urinary tract, including prostatitis, urethritis, and cystitis
- spinal tumors
- certain medications, especially psychotropic drugs, which are used to treat certain mental conditions or insomnia; antihypertensives, used to treat high blood pressure; and anticoagulants, used to thin the blood.

If you have an erection that is painful or lasts for more than 6 hours, you should see a doctor. If not treated early enough, priapism can cause severe damage to the erectile tissue and scar tissue that builds up in the penis, which can ultimately lead to impotence. The most common emergency treatment option is injection of medications that help shrink blood vessels, after withdrawing stagnant blood from the penis using a hollow needle attached to a syringe. When priapism is associated with intracavernous injection, an oral medication may sometimes reduce the erection. When other treatments fail, surgery to remove the stagnant blood and to create a shunt may be required.

If the cause of your priapism isn't obvious (eg, a side effect from penile injection), or if the doctor isn't familiar with your medical history, he or she will need to take a complete history, physical examination, and basic laboratory tests to make an accurate diagnosis. As with impotence, it's important to find the cause of priapism to treat it effectively and prevent recurrence (Table 1).

Peyronie's Disease

Peyronie's disease is a curvature in the penis, noticeable during an erection, that is caused by a buildup of plaque or scar tissue inside the penis in the lining of the

Table 1: Causes of Priapism

- Perineal or penile injury
- Light general anesthesia
- Medication: anticoagulants, psychotropics, anticonvulsants, androgens
- Procedure: intracavernous injection of vasodilators, hyperalimentation
- Diseases: sickle cell disease or trait, leukemia, multiple myeloma, urinary tract inflammation or infection
- Neurologic: spinal injury

corpora cavernosa. Named after the French surgeon who first reported it, Peyronie's disease affects about 1% of adult males. It generally affects men 40 to 60 years of age, but is occasionally reported in patients in their teens, and in their 80s.

Peyronie's disease may be painful, especially during an erection, and the curvature may be so severe that intercourse is impossible. In addition to the curvature, some other symptoms include painful erections, soft erections, and a lump under the skin of the penis. Unfortunately, doctors are not certain what causes the plaque to form, but many believe that it develops as a result of disease, medications, or trauma to the penis (Table 2). Peyronie's disease is not sexually transmitted and it is not cancer, although, in rare cases, the presence of a tumor may be confused with Peyronie's disease. To rule out the possibility of a malignancy, your doctor may want to perform a biopsy, especially if the plaque has grown rapidly.

Table 2: Proposed Causes of Peyronie's Disease

- Medical: venereal disease, arteriosclerosis, diabetes mellitus, phlebitis
- Pharmacologic: barbiturates, beta-blockers, vitamin E deficiency
- Familial: associated with Dupuytren's contracture of hands
- Traumatic: sexual excess, delamination injury
- Autoimmune: altered response to vascular trauma

A number of methods are used to treat Peyronie's disease, but their effectiveness is unpredictable. In some cases, particularly when the symptoms are mild and don't worsen with time, the condition will resolve without treatment, but it may take several years. If your symptoms are mild, the doctor may suggest that you give the symptoms a chance to improve on their own. If they persist, are painful, or make intercourse very difficult, you may need treatment.

Nonsurgical treatments (Table 3) should be tried first. If your condition is painful, the doctor will probably prescribe an oral pain medication. Oral medications may also be used to soften and reduce the plaque. Vitamin E, in doses of 400 to 1,000 units a day, is often tried first because it is inexpensive and safe. Other oral medications may be used, but they are generally effective in less than 50% of patients, and they are often associated with unpleasant side effects. Medication may also be injected directly into the plaque to soften and dissolve it, but the effectiveness of this treatment is also unpredictable.

Table 3: Common Agents for Peyronie's Disease

Oral	Dose	Action
Vitamin E	800 IU/d	Enhancing vasodilation and inhibit platelet aggregation; antioxidant
Potaba®	12 mg/d	Increases oxygen utilization at the tissue level; enhances the enzyme MAO activity, which decreases serotonin effect
Procarbazine	100 mg/d	Cytotoxic agent; MAO inhibitor
Tamoxifen	40 mg/d	Increases the secretion of TGF-β, (?) which decreases the inflammatory response and fibrogenesis
Colchicine	2.4 mg/d	Antitubulin; decreases collagen synthesis and induces collagenase activity
Verapamil	10 mg every 2 weeks for 12 injections	Inhibits scar formation, increases breakdown of fibrous tissue
Interferon	1 to 3 million U weekly for 3-5 weeks	Inhibits scar formation

Success*	Side effects
0%-91%	None
16%-88%	Stomach upset (32 tablets/day)
10%-56%	Leukopenia, thrombocytopenia, GI upset, germinal epithelial damage
55%	Reduced libido, facial flushing, reduced ejaculatory volume
37%-78%	Diarrhea, stomach upset, bone marrow suppression
0%-54%	Ecchymosis, temporary decrease in penile sensation
4%-60%	Influenza-like symptoms

*Reduction of curvature or size of plaque.

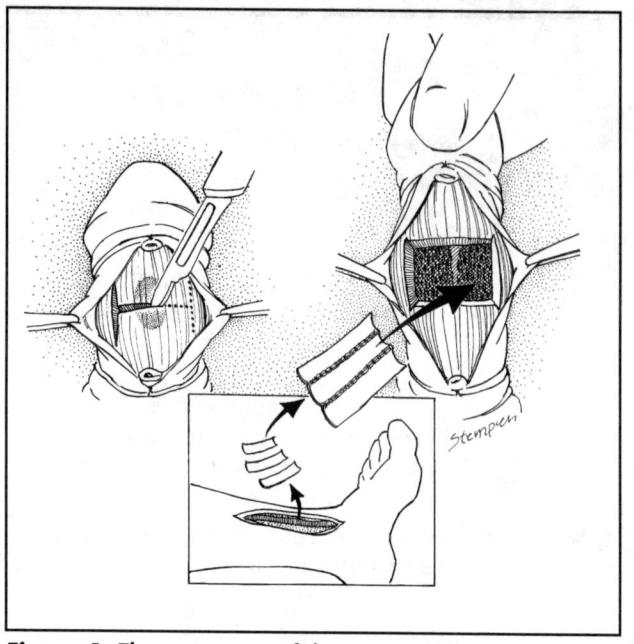

Figure 1: *The main steps of the venous patch graft surgery for correction of penile deformity. Note the use of the lower saphenous vein as graft material.*

Surgical treatments may involve cutting the plaque and repairing the area with a skin or vein graft (Figure 1); straightening the penis by shortening the unaffected side (Figure 2); or implanting a prosthesis to straighten the penis and provide enough rigidity for intercourse. In some cases your doctor may use a combination of treatments to correct the problem. Unfortunately, even after treatment, Peyronie's disease may return and become a chronic problem. You should discuss all the risks and potential complications with your doctor before selecting a treatment.

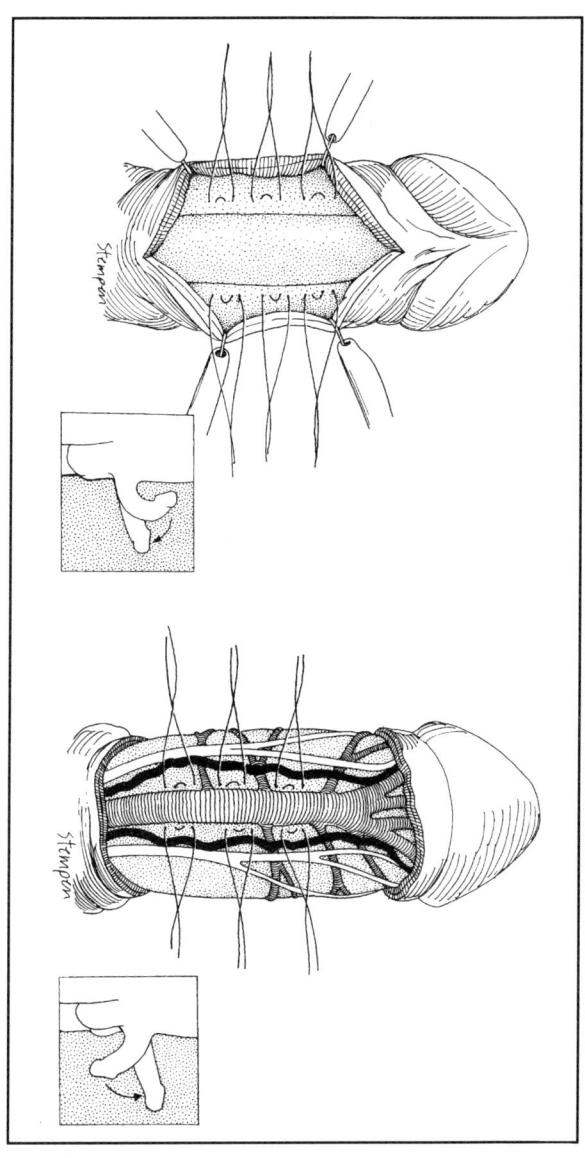

Figure 2: Straightening the penis by surgically using sutures to correct the abnormal curvature.

Chapter **6**

Finding the Right Doctor

A number of medical specialists have the appropriate background and training to treat erectile dysfunction (ED). However, if you have a personal physician—probably an internist or family practitioner—it is usually preferable to begin there. If your doctor doesn't feel comfortable treating ED or, after a preliminary evaluation, doesn't feel comfortable to provide suitable treatment, he or she may refer you to a urologist, endocrinologist, psychiatrist, or other appropriate specialist.

If you're new to an area and haven't found a personal physician yet; if you're not satisfied with your current doctor; or if you question your doctor's diagnosis or recommended treatment and want to get a second opinion, you can use any of a number of resources. Start by collecting a list of names, but you'll first want to decide whether you want a male or female doctor. Generally, this is a personal preference. You might want to begin your search by talking with friends and associates who can recommend doctors based on their own personal experiences. You will want to find out why they particularly liked the doctor, how difficult it is to get an appointment, the average length of time the doctor generally spends with each

64

patient, and how promptly the doctor returns a call if you have a medical question.

The local hospital also may be a resource. Many hospitals have special services that offer assistance in finding a doctor. The local or county medical association is another excellent resource for obtaining the names of physicians who practice in your area, as is the American Medical Association (AMA). You can find their numbers in the local phone book or by calling directory assistance. The AMA also has a reference book, the *American Medical Directory*, which is available at the library, along with other directories that list physicians. The Internet is another source for physician names. A number of Internet web sites offer help in finding a physician, including an AMA site. No matter where you get physicians' names, accessibility is important. Your list should only include doctors whose offices are accessible to your home or office.

When you have the names of several doctors who seem to meet your requirements, call their offices. Introduce yourself and explain that you are looking for a physician. You will probably talk with a receptionist or medical assistant, but this person should be willing and able to answer your questions. Be sure to note the receptionist's attitude and tone of voice. Is it friendly and concerned? Are your questions answered willingly and directly? The way you are greeted and how your questions are answered will give you a good sense of how 'patient-friendly' the medical office is. You may want to ask some of these questions:

- What hospital(s) is the doctor associated with?
- What are the office hours?
- What is the fee schedule—for a physical examination; for routine office visits?

65

- How does the office handle emergency situations, especially those that occur after office hours?
- How much time does the doctor allow for each appointment?
- What health insurance plans or health management organizations is the doctor affiliated with? This is especially important if your insurance carrier restricts your choice of doctors.

Based on what you learn from these phone interviews, and your instincts, you should be able to narrow your list to two or three physicians. Although it's not always possible, try to make an appointment for a brief meeting with each of the selected physicians. When you call for the appointment, explain that you are looking for a physician and would like a brief consultation. You may be expected to pay for the doctor's time, but it is a worthwhile investment, especially if you expect to build a long-term relationship with this person. During the consultation visit, you will want to note the atmosphere in the office. Is it clean, comfortable, and cheerful? Are the office personnel friendly? How crowded is the office? How long do you have to wait before you actually get to see the doctor?

When you meet with the doctor, remember that the purpose of your visit is to seek information that will help you choose a physician you can feel comfortable with and have confidence in. You need to answer some of these questions:

- Is this doctor qualified by both education and experience?
- Does he or she care about you as a person?
- Do you feel comfortable and relaxed when talking with him or her?

- Are you encouraged to ask questions?
- Do you understand the answers to your questions?
- Does the doctor speak in lay terms, or use medical jargon?
- Does the doctor seem relaxed in your presence?
- Does the doctor make you feel rushed? Does the doctor sit down to talk with you, or does he or she stand 'with one foot out the door?'

About Certification

In gathering information about physicians, you may find information that indicates a doctor is 'board certified' in a specialized area. For example, a doctor may be certified in geriatrics, urology, or family practice. This means that a doctor has demonstrated a certain amount of knowledge in a specialized area of medicine by passing a written examination administered by specialists practicing in the same field. A licensed physician does not have to be certified to practice a specialty, and certification by a medical specialty board doesn't automatically guarantee excellence. In fact, many excellent, highly respected physicians are not board certified. However, board certification does assure you that the doctor has some level of experience and knowledge in a particular specialty.

Expectations and Responsibilities

Ideally, the physician-patient relationship should be a partnership, but this isn't always easy. As a patient, you should have a number of expectations of your doctor. For example:
- You expect your doctor to provide as much information as possible about your specific illness or condition.

- You expect to be given a reasonable amount of time to ask questions and discuss concerns.
- You expect your physician to maintain your confidentiality, realizing that he or she may have to release your medical records to a consulting specialist. In addition, for some conditions—generally infectious diseases—your doctor is required, by law, to notify government authorities.
- You expect to participate in decisions about your care.
- You expect to have reasonable access to your doctor, based on the needs of your medical condition and the doctor's schedule.
- You expect to know where to obtain emergency care if your doctor is unavailable.
- You expect your doctor to see you within a reasonable time of your scheduled appointment.
- You expect to be able to change physicians at any time, and have your medical information promptly forwarded to your new physician.

Communication between you and your doctor is not a one-way street. Your doctor also has certain expectations of you so he or she can give you the best possible care. To fulfill those expectations, you have a number of responsibilities. First, you have a responsibility to provide your doctor with all information that might be related to your illness. This includes information about your medical history, your family, and your home and work environment that, although it may seem completely unrelated, may have an important impact on your health. To be sure that you get what you need from your doctor, and to expedite your visit, you should go over your questions ahead of time. If you don't understand something the doctor says during your visit, it is your responsibility to ask for an explanation. Also, don't forget the small courtesies, such as being on time for your appointment and giving 24 hours' notice if you have to cancel.

You are also responsible for accurately following the treatment your doctor prescribes. If for some reason you cannot, you should let your doctor know because you may be able to try an alternative treatment. Treatments often require time to take effect, so you need to be patient; however, if your symptoms worsen, if complications develop, or if you have an adverse effect from the medication, contact your doctor promptly.

Changing Physicians

Hopefully, the doctor you select will meet your expectations and you will maintain a long-term relationship. Remember that building confidence and trust takes time, so don't get in the habit of jumping from physician to physician because of a minor annoyance or misunderstanding. Under some circumstances, you should consider changing doctors. For example, if your doctor puts you off or seems annoyed by reasonable questions, you may want to consider finding another doctor. A good physician will welcome your questions and encourage you to take an active role in your health care.

You may discover a basic incompatibility between you and your doctor. If you sense this is happening, ask yourself some basic questions:

- Are you uncomfortable talking with your doctor about the personal aspects of your illness or your life?
- Do you feel that your doctor isn't always honest and straightforward with you?

- Do you frequently feel that your doctor isn't giving you his or her complete attention?
- Are your appointments often rushed?
- Is your doctor often unavailable, or is there a lack of after-hours coverage?
- Does your doctor tend to be patronizing or abrupt?
- Does your doctor fail to follow through on problems when they occur?

If the answer to many, or all, of these questions is 'yes,' it may be time to change physicians.

Second Opinions

If you have questions about your doctor's diagnosis or a treatment recommendation, don't hesitate to seek a second opinion. In fact, getting a second opinion has almost become standard practice in this age of rapidly expanding medical technology and high cost of many medical treatments. Also, some health insurance providers require a second opinion before approving certain surgical procedures.

Sometimes, your physician may suggest seeking a second opinion. A good doctor who is unsure about a diagnosis won't hesitate to refer you to a specialist, and may even be glad to have the diagnosis confirmed by another doctor. If you request a second opinion, don't try to hide it from your doctor. Let your doctor know that you would like to seek a second opinion before making a decision about treatment. Because your doctor's primary concern is to ensure your continued good health, he or she should understand and even welcome your request for a second opinion. If your doctor doesn't understand, then maybe he or she isn't the right doctor for you.

Chapter 7

Patient Case Studies

The following case studies are typical examples of the problems presented by patients in recent years and the steps taken to help them.

Obesity and erectile dysfunction

Mr. C, 49, gradually developed erectile dysfunction over 2 years. He had a history of high blood pressure and was taking several medications. However, his high blood pressure was still poorly controlled and his doctor had recently changed his medication. His physical examination revealed an obese man with a somewhat shrunken penis. He was actually unable to see his penis because of his large abdomen. He had used 50 mg of sildenafil (Viagra®) on two occasions but was not satisfied because it did not produce a satisfactory erection. On further questioning, it was revealed that he had a few problems in taking the medication. First, he took sildenafil directly after dinner, and then had some fears because of the publicity of deaths associated with its use.

He was instructed to take sildenafil on an empty stomach 1 hour before sexual intercourse. A few months later the patient came back for a follow-up visit and reported that on taking 100 mg of sildenafil on an empty stomach he was able to produce a reasonably good erection. However, during a work-up for mild chest pain he was diagnosed to have mild coronary arterial insufficiency. Because of fear of the side effects from the combined use of sildenafil and some cardiac drugs, his wife insisted that he not take the sildenafil anymore. The patient then wanted to try penile injection therapy. However, he was unable to see his penis and could not place the needle properly, even with a mirror. His wife came to the office on the next visit. She was a very attractive and dominant woman who stated that her husband was 'like a little boy' and she had to take care of everything for him. She said that she would perform the injection for him. After instruction, she performed penile injections on her husband with excellent results. The couple has been using penile injections without incident for the past 6 months.

Comment. In obese patients and patients with needle phobia, penile injection by the partner is an effective way of solving erectile problems. In fact, sexual partners often enjoy participation in the process.

Diabetes and erectile dysfunction

Mr. D, 35, had diabetes since he was 10 years old. He had been using insulin injections for 15 years and had an insulin pump implanted in his abdomen. He was depressed because of problems associated with his diabetes, especially impotence. He underwent a sleep erection study that showed borderline erectile ability. He occasionally had the sensation of pins and needles in his feet. Sildenafil (Viagra®) slightly improved his erections, but he was dissatisfied. A penile injection test showed excellent blood circulation in the penis.

Comment. Roughly half of all patients with diabetes suffer from erectile dysfunction. In younger men, this is caused by either psychological or nerve dysfunction. In older men, diabetes is often compounded by circulation problems or atrophy of the penile tissue. In mild cases, sildenafil (Viagra®) can be quite successful. However, if the patient's nerve is damaged or if his circulation is poor, more invasive treatments, such as penile injection or a vacuum device, or even a penile prosthesis, are required. For diabetic patients, better control of blood sugar levels improves the condition but is not a cure. Researchers are looking into ways to slow the progression of diabetes and provide better treatments for millions of patients with the disease.

Diabetes and heart drugs

Mr. M was 55 years old and had type II diabetes for 7 years. He was health conscious, watched his diet, and regularly took medication for diabetes and high cholesterol. He was slightly overweight and had been trying to exercise more often to lose weight. However, because of a back injury 10 years earlier he was unable to run or to play sports. He walked a mile or two each day. His eye doctor told him he had a mild degree of retinopathy (an eye disease that often occurs in patients with diabetes). He also experienced occasional numbness in his feet, which his doctor said might indicate peripheral neuropathy (damaged nerves in the legs and feet).

He had a mild heart attack about a year before. He took nitroglycerine, a drug used for chest pain, several times about 9 months earlier, but had not used it since. Nevertheless, he kept a bottle of it in a drawer just in case. A recent stress test was normal. He had been married for 30 years and had 2 grown children. He complained of gradual onset and progressive erectile dysfunction over the last 2 years. Because of his needle phobia (he passed out during a penile erection test in the doctor's office) he had been using a vacuum device with moderate success, but his wife complained that it was too mechanical. He had heard about sildenafil (Viagra®), but his wife would not let him try it because of fears about its side effects when used with certain cardiac drugs. He asked his doctor if sildenafil would be dangerous for him.

Comment. Although a number of deaths associated with sildenafil have been reported to the U.S. Food and Drug Administration, the drug has been shown to be safe for most men, except in those: (1) taking nitroglycerine or related drugs; (2) who have had a recent heart attack or stroke; (3) who have poor exercise tolerance, eg, unable to walk 3 flights of stairs; or (4) with a rare eye disease called retinitis pigmentosa.

Because Mr. M had recently passed a stress test, walked a mile or two a day, and was not taking nitroglycerine, Viagra® is not contraindicated. Nevertheless, I emphasize to patients the danger of taking Viagra® and nitroglycerine together. I would also ask the patient to inform his cardiologist and get permission before starting sildenafil so the cardiologist knows what to do in case of a heart attack. If the patient suffers chest pains again he will likely reach for the nitroglycerine, and this can be deadly if he has taken sildenafil within the past 24 hours.

Penile injury

Mr. P, 55, complained that acute onset of erectile dysfunction had begun 8 months earlier. The condition started when he suffered a penile injury during sexual intercourse. His wife was in the superior position when his penis slipped out and was compressed by his wife's pelvic bone. He heard a 'snapping' sound from his penis and it was painful for about half an hour. The penis became swollen and he also noticed several drops of blood coming from the meatus (tip of penis). He saw a doctor the next day and was treated with pain medication. He then was able only to get a soft erection, not sufficient to have sexual intercourse. An unrelated examination revealed high blood cholesterol, for which he was taking medication.

Physical examination revealed a moderately overweight man without emotional distress. The rest of the examination was normal except that a 1/2-cm nodule was found near the base of the penis. A color ultrasound study revealed a moderate degree of arterial insufficiency, probably because of the high blood cholesterol level. A penile injection test produced a 50% erection, which he stated was similar to the unsatisfactory erections he was able to have in the last 8 months. The ultrasound study also revealed a moderate degree of venous leakage from the penis and an x-ray study revealed that blood leaked out from the corpus cavernosum to the corpus spongiosum of the penis.

The diagnosis was that Mr. P had an abnormal communication between the erectile body of the penis and the spongy tissue surrounding the urethra. After 3 months of watchful waiting, the symptoms did not improve and he was operated on to repair the abnormal communication. Three months after the operation he was able to achieve and maintain a rigid erection. However, once he started thrusting, his penis became soft. The urologist diagnosed that he might have a condition called pelvic steal syndrome and prescribed sildenafil (Viagra®). He was then able to sustain an erection during sexual intercourse.

Comment. Two interesting conditions occurred with this patient: penile fracture and pelvic steal syndrome.

Penile fracture is not uncommon. It typically occurs when a couple is engaged in intercourse, with the female in superior position (on top). Sometimes the penis slips out of the vagina and is crushed by the woman's pelvis. Many couples have reported hearing a snapping sound from the penis. In mild cases, the pain lasts only a few minutes and the patient suffers a minor tear of the tunica, the covering of the erectile tissue. The tear typically heals naturally without any impairment of erectile function.

In more severe injuries, two situations may occur: erectile dysfunction or a nodule forms in the penis resulting in a penile deformity. In the latter, the scarring of the tunica albuginea may be minor and the patient will just feel a small lump. But in some patients, this may progress to Peyronie's disease (severe penile curvature), pain during erection, and penile deviation or narrowing. If the condition is seen early, the doctor may prescribe colchicine or vitamin E to suppress the inflammation. However, if it turns into full-blown Peyronie's disease with severe deformity, surgery may be necessary. In patients with severe fracture of the penis and blood leakage from the erectile body, immediate surgery is the best treatment. If this is not done, many patients will develop erectile dysfunction and severe scarring of the erectile tissues. The problem is caused by the inability of the tunica to keep the blood within the erectile tissue, a condition called venous leakage. In Mr. P's case, he was bleeding from the tip of the penis, indicating injury to the urethra and the surrounding tissue called the corpus spongiosum. This usually results in abnormal communication between the corpus cavernosum and the corpus spongiosum. Surgery is the only treatment.

Pelvic steal syndrome is an interesting condition. It usually occurs in patients with a history of high blood pressure, high cholesterol, or aortic aneurysm. The patient is usually able to achieve a satisfactory erection, but cannot maintain it during intercourse and pelvic thrusting. This is caused by a partial blockage of the arteries that supply blood to the pelvis, penis, buttocks, and lower legs. The amount of blood is sufficient to achieve an adequate erection during sexual stimulation, but once sexual intercourse begins and more blood is needed for the activity of the muscles in the buttocks and lower extremities, the penis becomes limp. In mild cases, medical treatment is usually helpful. In severe cases, vascular surgery or angioplasty may be required to open the partially blocked arteries.

Prostate cancer and erectile dysfunction

Mr. R was a 53-year-old CEO of a Silicon Valley company. His blood tests showed an elevated prostate specific antigen (PSA) level, and, after a prostate biopsy, he was diagnosed with prostate cancer. He consulted a dozen urologists from around the country and decided to have a radical prostatectomy, which is surgical removal of the cancerous prostate.

Six months after the operation he consulted me. He was disappointed and angry because his erection had not returned. He had good continence and no urinary problems. He had expected to have a complete recovery of his erectile function after 6 months because that's what he read on the Internet. He had tried sildenafil several times without success. He got a slight swelling of the penis during masturbation. He described his orgasms as painful and unpleasant. He had no ejaculation during orgasm. For the last 2 months he had been using penile injections to achieve erections, but developed a tenderness and a slight deviation of the penis after the injections. Before the prostate surgery he had sex 3 or 4 times a week and enjoyed a very satisfying sex life. He also worried that his penis seemed to have lost 1 inch since the operation.

Comment. Prostate cancer is one of the most common cancers in men. Since the invention of nerve-sparing radical prostatectomy by Dr. Patrick Walsh at Johns Hopkins University, many men have had this surgery and become free of cancer for many years. Before the nerve-sparing operation, 95% to 100% of patients became impotent after surgery and never recovered erectile function. The outcome from the nerve-sparing operation is much better, with 50% to 60% of men able to recover erectile function 6 to 24 months after the surgery. With the introduction of sildenafil (Viagra®), the percentage is expected to rise. Most men recover potency and continence, but others suffer from complications such as persistent incontinence, impotence, curving, scarring, and shortening of the penis. A small study in Italy showed that if patients start penile injections shortly after the prostate cancer operation they recover erectile function faster and more completely. In older men with vascular disease, a prolonged period of disuse of the penis could decrease chances of recovery because of atrophy of the penile muscles and blood vessels.

Incontinence is another major problem for prostate surgery patients. Patients are usually taught Kegel exercises shortly after surgery to improve bladder control. If the incontinence persists, some patients may benefit from the injection of collagen into the bladder neck. If the incontinence is severe, an artificial sphincter, a device that constricts the urethra, can be placed to control the urine leak.

Painful orgasms occur in some patients and are probably caused by the altered activity of the nerve system and spasm of the vas deferens during orgasm. In a small study in Chicago, about half the patients given α-blockers felt minimal or no pain during orgasm. This condition improves with time as the body adjusts to the altered anatomy. Shortening of the penis, as well as scar formation and curvature (Peyronie's disease), have been reported in some cases. The cause is unknown, but patients feel distressed when the penis becomes shorter or curved after a prostate operation.

In response to these complications, researchers in several institutions are exploring the possibility of using growth factors or gene therapy to speed the recovery of continence or sexual potency after radical prostatectomy. The idea is to use genes or growth factors shortly after surgery that are known to grow new blood vessels and new nerves. In animal experiments, rats have shown a remarkable recovery from nerve and arterial injury after being treated with growth factors.

Pituitary tumor and erectile dysfunction

Mr. J, a 59-year-old father of 3, complained of gradual onset of erectile dysfunction for 6 years. He also reported that he did not have much interest in sex because his wife was not as attractive to him anymore. He described his erections as partial and able to penetrate with some difficulty. His health was otherwise normal; he did not smoke or drink, exercised regularly, and his family history was negative for diabetes mellitus or endocrine disorders. Because of his history of declining sexual interest, we obtained a blood test for male hormones. It revealed very low levels of the male hormone, testosterone, and a high level of the pituitary hormone, prolactin. A brain magnetic resonance imaging (MRI) revealed a large tumor in his pituitary gland. The tumor was surgically removed and his testosterone level and sexual interest returned to normal levels. His erection improved, but not to 100%. However, he began taking sildenafil (Viagra®) and was then able to function sexually as well as when he was 20 years old.

Comment. The pituitary gland is a special area in the brain that controls the function of several hormone-producing glands in the body, such as thyroid, adrenal, and testicle (or ovary in female). A tumor in the pituitary gland may either destroy the cells that control the testicle or produce too much prolactin. Both of these conditions may cause decreased sexual interest and erectile dysfunction. When the tumor is large, it may invade the adjacent brain structures and threaten the patient's life. Therefore, a hormone test is an important part of the diagnostic process, especially when a man complains of loss of sexual interest.

Venous leakage

Mr. T, a 34-year-old, married software engineer, had a lifelong history of erectile dysfunction. His wife was aware of his problem before marriage and had been very supportive. He had a normal sexual drive and engaged in sexual activity about 3 times a week. He was able to attain an erection of about 60% but could only achieve penetration 10% of the time. Medical history included circumcision at age 21 in an attempt to cure the dysfunction. He had also been unsuccessfully treated by several psychotherapists. A urologist offered to implant a penile prosthesis because other medical treatments could not help him. One day while surfing the Internet, he read an article about a surgery that cures venous leakage impotence, and he contacted a specialist for diagnostic testing. A penile ultrasound test, given after injection of an erection-producing drug, revealed excellent arterial flow, large venous outflow, and a partial erection similar to his erections at home. However, a penile x-ray after dye injection showed large venous leaks at the base of the penis. He underwent surgery to repair the leakage and within a few days began to experience excellent erections. Soon after the surgery he fathered a child.

Comment. Primary impotence is a condition in which a man has never been able to achieve and maintain a normal erection. There can be several causes: congenital or traumatic artery or nerve injury; congenital or traumatic venous leakage; micropenis; or severe penile deformity. Primary impotence can also be caused by psychological factors such as child abuse, rape, religious or moral strictures, or misinformation. A detailed medical and psychosexual history is mandatory to identify the cause and determine management strategy so that unnecessary psychotherapy and suffering can be avoided. Erectile dysfunction in a young adult can have a devastating effect on self-image and behavior development. For example, I have seen a high school senior who often displayed destructive behavior and had a criminal record. A social worker finally discovered that his self-destructive behavior was a result of his inability to attain a normal erection. After surgical repair of his venous leakage, his behavior completely changed and he went to a military academy and became an officer.

When I saw him again 5 years later for an unrelated reason, he had a steady girlfriend and was very happy with his sex life. Another young man quit a famous college during his sophomore year. His parents were stunned until the young man confessed that he was depressed because he was unable to attain a normal erection. After surgical repair of venous leakage, he became a different person and went back to college. Another young man with a similar condition decided to write a book based on his experience so that others will not need to suffer as many years as he did.

A misunderstanding

Mr. W was 23 years old and complained of the inability to achieve a 100% erection. He stated that about 2 years ago he began to notice that his erection was not like it used to be. He had no history of injury, was not married, and had no sexual partner. He masturbated about 6 times a week and complained that his ejaculate 'looked like water.' He was otherwise healthy. While in college he rode a bicycle daily for about 4 years. Further medical examination found no abnormalities. A hormonal workup was within normal limits and a Rigiscan study (to check his sleep erections) revealed several episodes of normal erections lasting more than 30 minutes. Interestingly, the patient also complained that he has no morning or night erections. A combined injection and stimulation test was performed with 10 µg of prostaglandin E_1. This resulted in a 100% rigid erection, pointing about 45 degrees upward. The erection lasted for about 40 minutes and gradually subsided. Mr. W stated that the erection produced by the injection was similar to his erections at home, but his erections used to be much harder.

Comment. Diagnosis: normal erection, misunderstanding of erectile physiology. I have seen several similar cases. This typically happens with men in their late teens and early 20s. Many young men think the penis should be rock hard at a moment's notice. Human erection has 2 phases: in the first phase the pressure is about 100 mm Hg, a little below the normal blood pressure of 120; the second phase occurs during masturbation or sexual intercourse when the penis is touched. This triggers the bulbo cavernous reflex that makes the muscle on the outside of the penis squeeze the base. At this point the penis is much harder and the pressure can go to several hundred mm Hg. This is the rigid erection phase that normally occurs. Teenagers, because of their high testosterone level and the sensitivity of the penis, tend to get this rock-hard erection more often. However, in adults, this occurs only during masturbation or sexual intercourse. Some young men think they should manifest the second phase of erection all the time, an obvious misunderstanding. This kind of erection problem only requires an explanation of the physiology and some assurance.

Trauma and erectile dysfunction

Mr. A, a 34-year-old carpenter, had been a political prisoner and a torture victim in his native country. One of the torture techniques involved having a woman confront him to arouse him and then applying electric rods to his erect penis. As a result of repeated tortures, Mr. A was unable for 10 years to attain and maintain an erection. He underwent extensive psychotherapy after arriving in the U.S. and was able to live a relatively normal life. His erection problem, however, persisted even after a year of sex therapy. His urologist gave him several treatments, including sildenafil (Viagra®), medicated urethral system for erection (MUSE®), a vacuum device, and penile injection, all without success. A nocturnal penile erection test confirmed that his erection problem was not psychological. He was referred to a specialist for a detailed evaluation. A penile ultrasound test showed severe penile arterial insufficiency, which was reaffirmed by a pudendal arteriography— an x-ray imaging of the arteries in the pelvic area done after dye is injected into the large abdomen artery. In bypass surgery, an artery from the stomach was removed to bypass the blocked segment of the penile artery. Mr. A's erections improved significantly after surgery but they were still not rigid enough to have sexual intercourse. However, he was able to have sex by using either Viagra® or MUSE®.

Comment. Sexual dysfunction is common in torture victims. Intensive psychosexual therapy is effective in many patients. However, if erectile dysfunction persists and is confirmed by nocturnal erection test, a detailed vascular evaluation should be performed. In this case, the cause of the patient's problem was blocked penile arteries from repeated electric shock injury.

Premature ejaculation

Mr. P was a 57-year-old teacher with a history of premature ejaculation, a condition that worsened in the last two years. Moreover, his erections were not as firm as they had been and often became flaccid during sexual intercourse. He was otherwise healthy and enjoyed an enduring relationship with his wife of 30 years. A physician prescribed sertraline (Zoloft®), an antidepressant drug occasionally used for premature ejaculation. This drug seemed to delay ejaculation for Mr. P by a minute or two, but seemed to worsen the erectile dysfunction. He was then given sildenafil (Viagra®), which helped sustain his erection but did not improve the premature ejaculation. His urologist recommended that Mr. P use penile injections that would make erections last much longer so that he could have sexual intercourse a second time to satisfy his wife. However, Mr. P feared the injections and requested another option.

Comment. Two types of premature ejaculation have been identified: primary and secondary. Primary usually occurs in younger men with little sexual experience. Their penises are very sensitive to touch or stroke and they have not learned how to control sexual excitement.

Secondary premature ejaculation usually occurs in older men who have begun to experience erectile dysfunction. Because they fear losing the erection, these men hurry and thrust harder and faster to maintain the erection. This results in their losing control of sexual excitement and actually ejaculating sooner.

In the 1970s, Masters and Johnson, the pioneer sex therapists, developed a stop-start technique to desensitize the penis. This involves a series of starting and stopping masturbation without ejaculation, combined with concentration on aspects of the sexual experience other than ejaculation. These exercises can help a man gain better control of the timing of ejaculation.

In addition to exercises like the stop-start approach, some antidepressant and antianxiety medications have been used to delay ejaculation, including Zoloft®, Prozac® (fluoxetine), Paxil® (paroxetine), and Anafranil® (clomipramine). These medications block the reuptake of serotonin in the brain, believed to have influence on the ejaculatory mechanism. Several trials have shown that these drugs can help some men with premature ejaculation. In my practice, men were not satisfied with the few minutes of delayed ejaculation that resulted when they took these drugs.

Instead, I found that a satisfying treatment for many men with premature ejaculation is applying a local anesthetic, EMLA® Cream (lidocaine and prilocaine), to the glans (head) of the penis. This topical cream, often given to children who are about to receive hypodermic needle injections, can be used to numb the skin of the penis head. The patient simply rubs the cream on the penis head, then waits 15 or 20 minutes before washing off the cream, just before engaging in sexual intercourse. The cream partially numbs the penis head, not enough to negate sexual pleasure, but enough to help the man perform intercourse much longer, often more than 30 minutes. The patient can adjust the degree of penile numbness by washing off the cream sooner, thus giving the anesthetic less time to be absorbed into the tissue.

More than 80% of my patients who suffer from premature ejaculation have expressed satisfaction with this treatment. However, in older men with erectile dysfunction *and* premature ejaculation, EMLA® may worsen the erectile dysfunction by reducing the sensitive feedback response (erogenous feeling) during intercourse. This feedback becomes more important in maintaining an erection when a man ages. In cases like this, combining the use of EMLA® and Viagra® will help a patient maintain an erection while also delaying ejaculation.

Conclusion

As stated in the Introduction, this book is not meant to substitute for a visit to your doctor. However, it can serve as a useful educational resource. At the very least, we hope the information in this book has helped you realize that your erectile dysfunction is not a cause for embarrassment. Your ability to perform sexually is not a measure of your masculinity. And, although you may *feel* alone, you are definitely not alone. As many as 30 million men in this country are struggling with the same problem, doubts, and fears that you are experiencing.

Armed with the knowledge this book has given you, we hope you now feel more comfortable about talking with your physician. Many treatment options are available, and more are on the horizon. If regaining sexual function is important to you, the chances are good that with patience and determination, you and your physician can find an appropriate solution.

Glossary

abdominal aneurysm—a ballooning of the aorta, the main artery to the heart.

andropause—'male menopause,' or the gradual decline in male hormones associated with aging.

arteriosclerosis—a thickening and loss of elasticity of the artery walls. Often referred to as 'hardening of the arteries.'

cGMP—a chemical produced during sexual stimulation that is instrumental in maintaining an erection.

corpora cavernosa—spongelike cylinders that run along the length of both sides of the penis. During sexual arousal, they fill with blood and expand, causing an erection.

external vacuum therapy—a treatment for impotence that involves drawing blood into the penis by creating a vacuum.

hyperthyroidism—a dysfunction of the thyroid gland characterized by the release of too much thyroid hormone.

hypogonadism—a severe deficiency of male hormone, which can cause impotence.

hypothyroidism—a dysfunction of the thyroid gland characterized by the release of too little thyroid hormone.

intracavernous injection—a drug therapy for treating impotence that involves injecting a drug into the side of the penis. The drug creates an erection by relaxing the smooth muscles and widening the blood vessels in the penis.

medicated urethral system for erection (MUSE®)—a treatment for impotence that involves depositing a tiny suppository directly into the urethra.

nocturnal penile tumescence (NPT)—a test to detect the presence of an erection during sleep.

PDE5—an enzyme found in the penis. It breaks down a chemical (cGMP) produced during sexual stimulation that is instrumental in maintaining an erection.

peripheral neuropathy—a loss of sensation in the extremities caused by damage to the nerves. It is a common complication of diabetes.

Peyronie's disease—a condition characterized by curvature of the penis, caused by the accumulation of plaque or scar tissue.

placebo—a preparation containing no medication that is used as a control in an experiment or test to determine the effectiveness of a drug.

plaque—a deposit of fatty material on the inner lining of an arterial wall, characteristic of atherosclerosis.

priapism—a persistent erection that is not associated with sexual arousal.

urethra—the passageway through which urine and semen are discharged.

venous leak—a condition that occurs when the veins in the penis do not adequately close off during erection. This allows blood to escape, reducing the erection.

Viagra®—the first oral medication designed specifically to treat impotence, approved by the FDA in March 1998; the generic name of the drug is sildenafil.

yohimbine—a natural aphrodisiac derived from the bark of the yohimbehe tree. Sometimes used to treat men with erectile dysfunction.

Index

A

α-adrenoceptor function 22
α-blockers 79
abdominal aneurysm 27
Accuform 50
aging 13, 14, 18
AIDS 13, 14
alcohol 17, 21, 25, 30, 31
alcoholism 13, 14
alprostadil 38, 39
Alzheimer's disease 13
Ambicor 50
American Medical Association
    (AMA) 65
AMS 600 50
AMS 600M 50
AMS 700 Ultrex 50
AMS 700 Ultrex Plus 50
AMS 700CX® 50
AMS 700CXM® 50
AMS Ambicor® 50
AMS Dynaflex® 50
Anafranil® 85
androgens 58
andropause 34
anesthesia 58
angina 18
angioplasty 77
anticoagulants 57, 58
anticonvulsants 58
antidepressants 16

antihypertensives 22, 36, 57
antitubulin 60
anxiety 11, 16, 18, 27, 31
anxiolytics 17
aortic aneurysm 77
Aphrodyne® 41
arterial insufficiency 72
arteriosclerosis 13, 59
atherosclerosis 46

B

barbiturates 59
beta-blockers 22, 59
bicycle injury 14
bicycle riding 31
bladder 9, 13
bladder cancer 50
bleeding disorder 44
blood count 27
blood sugar test 27
bone marrow suppression 60
bone marrow tumors 40
buttocks 77
bypass surgery 46

C

cardiac ischemia 36
cardiovascular disease 17
Caverject® 38
cavernous artery 10
changes in diet 31
chest pain 71, 73

cholesterol 20
cholesterol level 13, 27, 35, 73, 77
cigarette smokers 17
cigarettes 17
clomipramine (Anafranil®) 85
cognitive-behavioral therapy 32
colchicine 60, 76
colon 13
confidentiality 68
congestive heart failure 36
coronary disease 36
corpora cavernosa 8, 48
corpus cavernosum 9, 10, 75, 76
corpus spongiosum 10, 75, 76
Coumadin® 44
counseling/sex therapy 54
cyclic GMP 35
cystitis 57
cystoscopy 50

D

decreased sexual desire 34
delamination injury 59
depression 5, 11, 16, 18, 22, 27, 34
diabetes 12, 13, 14, 15, 20, 25, 35, 59, 72, 73
diabetes mellitus 59, 79
diarrhea 35, 60
diseases of blood vessels 12
dizziness 41
dorsal arteries 10
dorsal nerve 10

dorsal vein 10
drowsiness 34
drug abuse 30
drug-induced impotence 22
Dupuytren's contracture 59
Duraphase II 50
Duraphase® 48
Duraphase® penile prosthesis 48
Dynaflex 50

E

ecchymosis 60
Edex® 38
ejaculation 18, 43, 60
EMLA® Cream (lidocaine and prilocaine) 86
endocrinologist 23, 64
epilepsy 14
ErecAid® vacuum constriction device 45
erectile dysfunction (ED) 5, 16, 18, 20, 29, 52, 56, 64, 71, 73, 81, 85, 86
Esteem® vacuum constriction device 43, 45
exercise 31
external vacuum therapy 42

F

fatigue 5, 25
fear of failure 11, 32
fibrogenesis 60
fibrosis 54
fluoxetine (Prozac®) 85
flushing 35, 60

Food and Drug Administration (FDA) 40, 45, 74

G

gastrointestinal upset 60
glans 9
guilt 11, 33

H

head trauma 13
headache 35, 41
health insurance 53, 66
heart attack 18, 74
heart failure 18
heparin 44
high blood pressure 13, 16, 20, 25, 27, 35, 57, 71, 77
high cholesterol 13, 35, 73, 77
hormonal therapy 33
hormone replacement therapy (HRT) 34, 54
hot flashes 34
hypertension 17, 22, 41
hyperthyroidism 16
hypothyroidism 16

I

impotence 5, 9, 11, 13, 15, 23, 25, 34, 38, 56, 57, 78, 81
incontinence 78
indigestion 35
individual psychoanalytic therapy 31
inflatable implants 48
inhibition 32
injection therapy 53
insomnia 34, 57

insulin 15, 72
intercourse 62
interferon 60
intracavernous injection (ICI) 38, 39, 57, 58
intraurethral suppository 40
intraurethral therapy 41
irregular heartbeat 27
irritability 34
ischemia 36

K

Kegel exercises 78

L

lethargy 34
leukemia 40, 43, 56, 58
leukopenia 60
libido 54, 60
lidocaine 86
lipid profile 27
listlessness 34
liver dysfunction 18
liver function tests 27
low blood pressure 38
low self-esteem 11
low sex drive 33
lung disease 18
lupus 13

M

macular degeneration 37
magnetic resonance imaging (MRI) 80
male menopause 34
malleable devices 50
malleable implant 48, 53

marital conflict 11
masculinity 87
Masters and Johnson 85
masturbation 21, 83
mechanical implant 48
Mentor Acu-Form® 47, 50
Mentor Alpha-1 50
Mentor Mark II 50
monoamine oxidase (MAO)
   inhibitors 60
mood disorder 33
mood swings 34
multiple myeloma 58
multiple sclerosis 12, 13, 14
MUSE® (medicated urethral
   system for erection) 40, 54,
   83, 84
myeloma 58

N

nasal congestion 38
National Institutes of Health
   (NIH) 6
nausea 41
needle phobia 72, 73
nerve dysfunction 72
neuropathy 13
nitrates 35, 36
nitroglycerine 35, 73, 74
nocturnal penile tumescence
   (NPT) 27
nodule 76

O

obesity 71
orgasm 77, 79

P

pain 16, 38, 43
papaverine 38, 39
papaverine + phentolamine 39
papaverine + phentolamine +
   alprostadil 39
Parkinson's disease 13, 14
paroxetine (Paxil®) 85
Paxil® 85
pelvic fracture 14
pelvic steal syndrome 75, 77
pelvic surgery 12
pelvic trauma 14
penile curvature 76, 78
penile deformity 44
penile erection test 84
penile fracture 75
penile implant surgery 54
penile injection 54, 56, 73, 78,
   83
penile injection test 72, 75
penile injection therapy 72
penile injections 85
penile injury 58, 74
penile pain 43, 54
penile prosthesis 46, 47, 48,
   50, 73, 80
performance anxiety 32
peripheral neuropathy 73
Peyronie's disease 26, 44, 57,
   58, 62, 76, 79
phentolamine 38
phlebitis 59
pituitary gland 16
pituitary tumor 79

poor blood flow to the penis 12, 13, 15
Post-T-Vac system 45
Potaba® 60
premature ejaculation 84, 85, 86
prescription drugs 12, 16, 25
priapism 38, 39, 44, 54, 56, 57, 58
prilocaine 86
procarbazine (Matulane®) 60
prolactin 16, 80
prostaglandin E1 38, 82
prostate 9, 13
prostate biopsy 26
prostate cancer 16, 26, 34, 77, 78
prostate surgery 14, 35, 78
prostate ultrasound 26
prostate-specific antigen (PSA) 26
prostatectomy 44, 77, 78, 79
prostatitis 57
prostheses 50, 53, 62
Prozac® 85
psychiatrists 23, 64
psychologists 23
psychosexual therapy 31
psychosis 33
psychotherapy 83
psychotropic drugs 57, 58
pubic bone 9

R

radiation therapy 14
rapid heartbeat 38
renal (kidney) failure 13
retinitis pigmentosa 37, 74
retinopathy 73
Rigiscan study 82
ruptured disk 13

S

scar formation 60
scarring 13, 38, 76, 78
schizophrenia 39
scrotal pump 49
scrotum 49
sedation 17
serotonin 60, 85
sertraline (Zoloft®) 84
sex therapy 32
sexual desire 16
sexual drive 26
sexual dysfunction 31
sexual intercourse 36, 74, 75, 77, 83, 84
shortening of the penis 78, 79
sickle cell anemia 40, 43, 56
sickle cell disease 58
sickle cell trait 58
sildenafil (Viagra®) 34, 36, 71, 72, 73, 74, 75, 77, 78, 80, 83, 84
skin graft 62
smoking 21, 25, 30
spina bifida 13
spinal cord injury 12, 14
spinal injury 58
spinal tumors 57
stenosis 22
stomach ulcer 16

stomach upset 38, 60
stress 5, 11, 20, 21, 25
stroke 13, 74
stuffy nose 35
substance abuse 12, 17
suppository 40
sweaty palms 41
symptom-oriented therapy 32

T

tamoxifen (Nolvadex®) 60
tension 20
testes 49
testicle 80
testosterone 16, 18, 26, 33, 54, 79, 80
thrombocytopenia 60
transforming growth factor-β (TGF-β) 60
trauma 12, 13, 14, 83
tumor 13, 14, 58
tunica 76
tunica albuginea 76
type II diabetes 73

U

ulcers 41
ultrasound study 75
urethra 8, 9, 10, 40, 50, 76, 78
urethritis 57
urinalysis 27
urinary tract infections 57, 58
urologist 23, 64, 75, 77, 80, 83

V

vacuum constriction device 42, 43, 44, 45, 53, 54, 73, 74, 83
vascular disease 13
vascular surgery 46, 54
vascular trauma 59
vein graft 62
venereal disease 59
venous leakage 14, 75, 76, 80, 81, 82
verapamil 60
VET system 45
Viagra® 34, 35, 36, 37, 52, 54, 71, 72, 73, 74, 84, 86
vision changes 35
vitamin B_1 13
vitamin B_2 13
vitamin B_6 13
vitamin deficiencies 14
vitamin E 59, 60, 76
vitamin E deficiency 59
VTU system 45

W

weakness 34
wine 31

Y

Yocon® 41
yohimb tree 41
yohimbine 41
Yohimex™ 41

Z

Zoloft® 84, 85